I0440750

# ALSO BY ROB LOUGHRAN:

## FICTION:
Beautiful Lies
High Steaks
Norman Babbit, Scientist
Tantric Zoo
T.A.P.F.O.S.
Chakra Stories
The Bartender

## NON-FICTION:
Things I Wish I Did Not Know About Writing:
15 Essays on Dreams, Sorrows, and Proofreading

How to Write a Novel and Still Have Time for Sex

A Man walks Into a Bar….A Compendium of
Filthy, Uncouth, Lewd, Lusty, and Lascivious Jokes

A Fun, Filthy Jokebook: Part II

Tomorrow & Tomorrow & Tomorrow: A Year-
Long Program for Publishing Success

The Official Love & Marriage Jokebook

Stop me If You've Heard This One

A _____ Walks Into a Bar

The Official Nasty and Blasphemous Religious
Jokebook

The Official X-Rated Animal Jokebook

# YOU HAD BETTER GIVE A ****

906 Quotes By, For, and About the Writer

by

# Rob Loughran

## Introduction

No matter how intense or honest or pure our desire to become a writer it ultimately comes down to having talent, developing your particular level of talent, or giving up.  And it doesn't matter what the public is reading, what Oprah is recommending, or how you feel.

If you are a writer you'll start writing that book and you'll finish it.  Then whether it sells or not—whether it's published or not—you'll finish another.

And another.

And another.

If you don't you're not a writer.

This isn't a particularly comfortable or encouraging proposition and the fact that it might result in a lifetime of toil that ends in debt and obscurity doesn't, however unfair, make it any less true.  When I seriously considered quitting writing I realized the crater left behind could never be filled with familial bliss, money, Irish whiskey, or vacations. In the end it doesn't matter if my books are bestsellers or any-kind-of-sellers; it only matters that they be written.

Anything less would be a waste of my life.

God help me, I'm a writer.

And, God help me again, reading little nuggets of wisdom from other writers are sometimes the only thing that gets me to scribble another word, sentence, or paragraph.

Pathetic, but here are 906 of my favorites.

## 1

There are no rules to writing, but if there were, caring would be right up there. Or, as we intellectuals are fond of saying, you had better give a shit.

—William Goldman

## 2

Writing is a job. Do it well and it is a great life. Mess around and its disappointments will kill you.

—James Michener

## 3

If you haven't always been doing it, you haven't always wanted to do it.

—George V. Higgins

## 4

If it sounds like writing, I rewrite it.

—Elmore Leonard

## 5

The state that you need to write is the state that others are paying large sums of money to get rid of.

—Shirley Hazzard

## 6

In today's book market, writers can't just be writers. They have to be performers and publicists as well. The image of the lonely writer honing his or her art is fast becoming outdated. What's demanded instead is something else: a hook, a smile, a shoeshine.

—Joshua Henkin

7

A real writer learns from earlier writers the way a boy learns from an apple orchard—by stealing what he has a taste for and can carry off.

--Archibald MacLeish

8

You should write, first of all, to please yourself. You shouldn't care a damn about anybody else at all. But writing can't be a way of life; the important part of writing is living. You have to live in such a way that your writing emerges from it.

—Doris Lessing

9

But I discovered when I was very young, before I was in my teens, that nothing could so quickly cast doubt on, and even destroy, an author's character's as bad dialog. If the people did not talk right, they were not real people. The closer to real talk, the closer to real people....A man or woman who does not write good dialog is not a first-rate writer.

—John O'Hara

10

What interests one in a novel...is the quantity of glimpsed detail, the asides and the incidents along the way; not the over-all turn of events or the holocaust at the close or the happy ending.

—Thornton Wilder

11

Advice from this elderly practitioner is to forget publishers and just roll a sheet of copy paper into your machine and get lost in your subject. Write about it by day and dream about it at night.

—E.B. White

12

The price we pay for money is paid in liberty.

—R.L. Stevenson

### 13

Poets don't write to be understood.

—Richard Feynman

### 14

If your morals make you dreary, depend on it, they are wrong.

—R.L. Stevenson

### 15

For me, words are a form of action capable of influencing change.

—Ingrid Bengis

### 16

A real book is not one that we read, but one that reads us.

—W.H. Auden

### 17

That some good can be derived from every event is a better proposition than everything happens for the best, which it assuredly does not.

—James Kern Feibleman

### 18

Words are timeless. You should utter them or write them with knowledge of their timelessness.

—Kahil Gibran

### 19

A great secret of success is to go through life as a man who never gets used up.

—Albert Schweitzer

### 20

The most futile thing in this world is any attempt, perhaps, at exact definition of character. All individuals are a bundle of contradictions—none more so than the most capable.

—Theodore Dreiser

### 21

The quality of our thoughts is bordered on all sides by our faculty with language.

—J. Michael Stracynski

### 22

Every man's memory is his private literature.

—Aldous Huxley

### 23

The greatest analgesic, soporific, stimulant, tranquilizer, narcotic, and to some extent even antibiotic—in short, the closest thing to a genuine panacea—know to medical science is work.

—Thomas Szasz

### 24

To a poet, silence is an acceptable response, even a flattering one.

—Colette

### 25

Because if you are like most people, then like most people you don't know you are like most people.

—Daniel Gilbert

### 26

A work in which there are theories is like an object which still has its price-tag on it.

—Marcel Proust

### 27

One must be drenched in words, literally soaked in them, to have the right ones form themselves into the proper patterns at the right moment.

—Hart Crane

### 28

As a writer I believe that all the basic human truths are known. And what we try to do as best we can is come at these truths from our own unique angle to reilluminate those truths in a hopefully different way.

—William Goldman

### 29

The secret of health for both mind and body is not to mourn for the past, not to worry about the future, or not the anticipate troubles, but to live the present moment wisely and earnestly.

—Buddha

### 30

The moment a writer picks up his pen, he is no longer himself or entirely of this world.

—Richard Selzer

### 31

I believe entertainment can aspire to be art, and can become art, but if you set out to make art you're an idiot.

—Steve Martin

### 32

We just can't make the best of a fate until it is inescapably, inevitably, and irrevocably ours.

—Daniel Gilbert

### 33

When we open our eyes each morning, it is upon a world we have spent a lifetime learning to see. We are not given the world: we make our world through incessant experience, categorization, memory, reconnection.

—Oliver Sacks

### 34

Who controls the society's memory controls its will.

—Phillip J. Hilts

### 35

And, of course, any writer who pays attention to critics is an ass.

—John D. MacDonald

### 36

Words are loaded pistols.

—Jean-Paul Sartre

### 37

We lie the loudest when we lie to ourselves.

—Eric Hoffer

### 38

Tomorrow is promised to no one.

—Walter Payton

### 39

No right or wrong storytelling answer exists. *Ever.*

—William Goldman

### 40

If it was easy everyone would do it.

—Billie Jean King

### 41

Storytellers have been getting us through the night for centuries. Hollywood is the current campfire.

—Gloria Steinham

### 42

All living souls welcome whatever they are ready to cope with; all else they ignore or pronounce to be monstrous and wrong, or deny to be possible.

—George Santayana

### 43

Stability in language is synonymous with rigor mortis.

—Ernest Weekley

### 44

We are so accustomed to disguise ourselves to others that in the end we become disguised to ourselves.

—Francois duc de la Rouchefoucauld

### 45

Act as if what you do makes a difference. It does.

—William James

## 46

What is wanted is not the will to believe, but the will to find out, which is the exact opposite.

—Bertrand Russell

## 47

Names are codes; we should not let familiarity with them masquerade as understanding.

—P.W. Atkins

## 48

The point of all this is that the answer to "Where do you get the idea for a story?" depends completely on what the questioner means by "idea" and "story." I get first the idea that causes me to sit down and write. And when I see what I have written, I get the idea for the story that I send out.

—George V. Higgins

## 49

I shall argue that most of the words are empty of meaning at the deepest level of comprehension and that they have acquired apparent meaning in order to encapsulate phenomena and facilitate conservation.

—P.W. Atkins

## 50

The world is a story we tell ourselves about the world.

—Vikram Chandra

## 51

Right now I'm having amnesia and déjà vu at the same time. I think I've forgotten this before.

—Stephen Wright

## 52

I object to publishers: the one service they have done me is to teach me to do without them. They combine commercial rascality with artistic touchiness and pettishness, without being either good businessmen or fine judges of literature. All that is necessary in the production of a book is an audience and a bookseller, without the intermediate parasite.

—George Bernard Shaw

53

What matters is not the idea a man holds, but the depth at which he holds it.

—Ezra Pound

54

Language is the only homeland.

—Czeslaw Milosz

55

There is wisdom in turning as often as possible from the familiar to the unfamiliar: it keeps the mind nimble, it kills prejudice and fosters humor.

—George Santayana

56

Writing is finally about one thing: going into a room alone and doing it.

—William Goldman

57

I don't know why we are here but I'm pretty sure that it is not in order to enjoy ourselves.

—Ludwig Wittgenstein

58

I don't care what anyone says, we were put here to fuck around.

—Kurt Vonnegut

59

The truth is that our finest moments are most likely to occur when we are feeling deeply uncomfortable, unhappy, or unfulfilled. For it is only in such moments propelled by our discomfort, that we are likely to step out of our ruts and start searching for different ways or truer answers.

—M. Scott Peck

## 60

By no means all of the nation's 750,000 or so lawyers crave elevation to the 761 judgeships authorized by Congress to serve on all the courts of the United States, from district to Supreme, but those who do in all likelihood face less intimidating odds than would dissuade the writer toiling in obscurity.

—George V. Higgins

## 61

Lots of times you have to pretend to join a parade in which you're not really interested in order to get where you are going.

—Christopher Morley

## 62

No one means all he says and yet very few say all they mean for words are slippery and thought is viscous.

—Henry Brooks Adams

## 63

As far as I'm concerned "whom" is a word that was invented to make everyone sound like a butler.

—Calvin Trilling

## 64

Alas, after a certain age every man is responsible for his fate.

—Albert Camus

## 65

Trust is what the fiction writer needs from the reader, because the writer is trying to make the reader believe what both of them know in the abstract to be a pack of lies.

—George V. Higgins

## 66

The assholes are everywhere.

—Ross Thomas

## 67

Wit is educated insolence.

—Aristotle

## 68

What saves a man is to take a step. Then another step. It is always the same step, but you have to take it.

—Antoine de Saint Exupery

## 69

It doesn't hurt to be optimistic. You can always cry later.

—Lucimar Santos de las Lima

## 70

Do what you can, with what you have, where you are.

—Teddy Roosevelt

## 71

The total history of almost anyone would shock almost anyone.

—Mignon McLaughlin

## 72

I want to go on living even after my death! And therefore I am grateful to God for giving me this gift, this possibility of developing myself and writing, of expressing all that is in me. I can shake off everything if I write; my sorrows disappear, my courage is reborn.

—Anne Frank

## 73

To have courage for whatever comes in life—everything lies in that.

—St. Theresa of Avila

## 74

People say, "What is the sense of our small effort?" They cannot see that we must lay one brick at a time, take one step at a time.

—Dorothy Day

## 75

Nothing you ever write, if you hope to be good, will ever come out as you first hoped.

—Lillian Hellman

## 76

My purpose is to entertain myself first and other people secondly.

—John D. MacDonald

## 77

You have to protect your writing time. You have to protect it to the death because the easiest thing to do on earth is not write.

—William Goldman

## 78

The best years of your life are the ones in which you decide your problems are your own. You do not blame them on your mother, the economy, or the president; you realize that you control your own destiny.

—Albert Ellis

## 79

When I stepped from hard manual work to writing, I just stepped from one kind of hard work to another.

—Sean O'Casey

## 80

Try again. Fail again. Fail better.

—Samuel Beckett

## 81

The time to begin writing an article is when you have finished it to your satisfaction. By that time you begin to clearly and logically perceive what it is that you really want to say.

—Mark Twain

## 82

Anyone who tells you how to write bestsellers is a sham and a liar. I can tell you how I write books. I write them with fear, excitement, discipline and a lot of hard work.

—Danielle Steele

83

Let's get this straight right away: Writers write; everyone else makes excuses.

—Jack M. Bickham

84

Our only three options as writers? We can: 1) BE GOOD 2) GET GOOD or 3) QUIT. That's it.

—Rob Loughran

85

No passion in the world is equal to the passion to alter someone else's draft.

—H.G. Wells

86

I quote others only the better to express myself.

—Michel de Montaigne

87

I have made this letter longer than usual because I lack the time to make it short.

—Blaise Pascal

88

The little wheels of invention are set in motion by the damp hand of melancholy.

—James Thurber

89

The reason why so few books are written is that so few people who can write know anything.

—Walter Bagehout

90

Memory is not a dutiful scribe that keeps a complete transcript of our experiences, but a sophisticated editor that clips and saves key elements to rewrite the story each time we ask to reread it.

—Daniel Gilbert

## 91

Screenwriting is not something at which you necessarily improve: You may be as good as you're going to get your second or third time out.

—William Goldman

## 92

Know what's weird? Day-by-day nothing seems to change. But pretty soon everything's different.

—Bill Waterson

## 93

We all have talent. How we use it and don't use it is what the game is all about in writing and in life itself. We must not get beaten down by those who choose to simply take up space on this planet, by those whose lives risk counting for nothing.

—Lew Hunter

## 94

One writes out of one thing only—one's own experience. Everything depends on how relentlessly one forces from this experience the last drop, sweet or bitter, it can possibly give.

—James Baldwin

## 95

Artistic temperament is a disease that only afflicts amateurs.

—Sarah Bernhardt

## 96

I love work. Why, sir, when I have a piece of work to perform I go away to myself, sit down in the shade, and muse over the coming enjoyment. Sometimes I muse too long.

—Mark Twain

## 97

I love being a writer. What I can't stand is the paperwork.

—Peter DeVries

### 98

Modern English is the Wal Mart of languages: convenient, huge, superficially friendly, and devouring all rivals in its eagerness to expand.

—Mark Abley

### 99

Don't wrap characters in the same grammar blanket.

—William Noble

### 100

Reject your sense of injury and the injury itself disappears.

—Marcus Aurelius

### 101

Monsieur Flaubert is not a writer.

—*Le Figaro*'s review of *Madame Bovary*.

### 102

Poetry is a subject as precise as geometry.

—Flaubert

### 103

The most important advice I would suggest to beginning writers: *Try to leave out the parts that readers skip*.

—Elmore Leonard

### 104

Humor is the art of making someone laugh without making them puke.

—Steve Martin

### 105

A writer's problem does not change. He himself changes and the world he lives in changes but his problem remains the same. It is always how to write truly and having found what is true, to project it in such a way that it becomes a part of the experience of the person who reads it.

—Ernest Hemingway

### 106

The best mind altering drug is truth.

—Lily Tomlin

### 107

If a man wishes to be sure of the road he treads on, he must close his eyes and walk in the dark.

—St. John of the Cross

### 108

Most people die with their music still locked up inside them.

—Benjamin Disraeli

### 109

Rejection slips are living proof that I send my work forth, that I am being read, that I am casting my lot. They help define me to my writing self.

—Shelly Lowenkopf

### 110

Sit down and put down everything that comes into your head and then you're a writer. But an author is one who can judge his own stuff's worth, without pity, and destroy most of it.

—Colette

### 111

If I had more time, I would write a shorter letter.

—Blaise Pascal

### 112

Last winter I forced myself through his *Tale of Two Cities*. It was a sheer dead pull from start to finish. It all seemed so insincere, such a transparent make-believe, a mere piece of acting.

—John Burroughs on Charles Dickens

### 113

No one is useless in this world who lightens the burdens of another.

—Charles Dickens

### 114
Forever is composed of nows.

—Emily Dickinson

### 115
What you have experienced no power on earth can take from you.

—Anonymous

### 116
Finish everyday and be done with it. You have done what you could; some blunders and absurdities have crept in; forget them as soon as you can. Tomorrow is a new day; you shall begin it serenely and with too high a spirit to be encumbered with your old nonsense.

—Ralph Waldo Emerson

### 117
Humor is the great thing, the saving thing, after all. The minute it crops up, all our hardnesses yield, all our irritations and resentments flit away, and a sunny spirit takes their place.

—Mark Twain

### 118
We die only once and for such a long time.

—Moliere

### 119
Anyone can do any amount of work, provided it isn't the work he is supposed to be doing.

—Robert Benchley

### 120
I tend to get very suspicious of anything that thinks it's art while it's being created.

—Douglas Adams

### 121
You can spend your entire life writing and rewriting the same first chapter if you listen to other people's

opinions and ignore the one sure place where you will always find the truth: In your own body.

—Elizabeth George

122

We either make ourselves happy or miserable. The amount of work is the same.

—Carlos Castenada

123

Life shouldn't be printed on dollar bills.

—Clifford Odets

124

A living language is like a man suffering incessantly from small haemorrhages, and what it needs above all else is constant transactions of new blood from other languages.

—H.L. Mencken

125

To confront a person with his own shadow is to show him his own light.

—Carl Jung

126

Writing the last page of the first draft is the most enjoyable moment in writing. It's one of the most enjoyable moments in life, period.

—Nicolas Sparks

127

Genius means little more than the faculty of perceiving in an inhabitual way.

—William James

128

When we try to pick out anything by itself, we find it hitched to everything else in the universe.

—John Muir

129

The instruction that I hope you will get out of this, if you want to be a published writer, seems general and abstract, but in operation it is specific, material, and demanding. It is that you must pay attention at all times, especially when you do not want to pay attention and are somewhat impatient about what is going on, because irritation is nature's way of nudging us, and the incidents that irritate us are important.

—George V. Higgins

### 130

Here is a lesson in creative writing. First rule: do not use semicolons. They are transvestite hermaphrodites representing absolutely nothing. All they do is show you've been to college.

—Kurt Vonnegut

### 131

There is only one way to make money at writing, and that is to marry a publisher's daughter.

—George Orwell

### 132

The secret remains that there is no secret. The way to determine whether you have talent is to rummage through your files and see if you have written anything; if you have, and quite a lot, then the chances are you have the talent to write more. If you haven't written anything, you do not have the talent because you do not want to write. Those who do can't help themselves. We do it for the hell of it, and those who raise a lot of hell, and then get very lucky, well, we make a living, too. There are worse ways to travel through this vale of tears than by doing the things you love, and making a living at it.

—George V. Higgins

### 133

Conceal a flaw and the world will imagine the worst.

—Martial

### 134

Where is the wisdom we have lost in knowledge?
Where is the knowledge we have lost in information.

—T.S. Eliot

### 135

Nothing great is created suddenly.

—Epictetus

### 136

Words are like money. It is the stamp of custom
alone that gives them circulation or value.

—William Hazlitt

### 137

It is difficult to get the news from poems yet men
die miserably every day for lack of what is found there.

—William Carlos Williams

### 138

The reward for conformity was that everyone liked
you except yourself.

—Rita Mae Brown

### 139

They know enough who know how to learn.

—Henry Adams

### 140

You write a hit play the same way you write a flop.

—William Saroyan

### 141

Our deeds determine us, as much as we determine
our deeds.

—George Eliot

### 142

The girl, it doesn't seem to me, have a special
perception or feeling which would lift that book above
the curiosity level.

—Anne Frank's rejection slip for *The Diary of Anne
Frank*

### 143

The final forming of a person's character lies in his own hands.

—Anne Frank

### 144

If you want creative workers, give them time enough to play.

—John Cleese

### 145

The roots of language are irrational and of a magical nature.

—Jorge Luis Borges

### 146

One of the most difficult decisions an unpublished writer makes is when to take advice and when to ignore all your well-meaning critics and do it your way.

—Sue Grafton

### 147

Words form the thread on which we string our experiences.

—Aldous Huxley

### 148

I saw the angel in the marble and carved until I set him free.

—Michelangelo

### 149

I don't believe in detailed outlines because once a book has been outlined too rigidly, the rest is only typing—and that's no fun.

—Ed McBain

### 150

My play was a complete success. The audience was a failure.

—Ashleigh Brilliant

### 151

I don't think anybody remembers the truth, the facts. You remember impressions.

—Robert Altman

### 152

For me, words are a form of action, capable of influencing change.

—Ingrid Bengis

### 153

Bare lists of words are found suggestive to an imaginative and excited mind.

—Ralph Waldo Emerson

### 154

The great enemy of clear language is insincerity.

—George Orwell

### 155

You are what you believe.

—Anton Chekov

### 156

We cannot do without reality and we cannot do without illusion.

—Daniel Gilbert

### 157

To write a novel, you begin with what you can see and then you add what came before and what came after.

—Thomas Harris

### 158

Dictionaries are like watches: the worst is better than none, and the best cannot be expected to go quite true.

—Samuel Johnson

### 159

Writing is a many-faceted craft. It requires imagination, precision, clarity, a sense of reality, a sense of fun. At times it demands a scientist's accuracy, at other times a con man's charm. More often than not it necessitates a combination of the two.

—Gene Perret

160

The sum of human wisdom is not contained in any one language, and no single language is capable of expressing all forms and degrees of human comprehension.

—Ezra Pound

161

If you can speak what you will never hear, if you can write what you will never read, you have rare things.

—Thoreau

162

Nobody, including the Supreme Court, knows what obscenity is.

—Norman Dorsen

163

An eccentric, dreamy, half-educated recluse in an out-of-the-way New England village—or anywhere else—cannot with impunity set at
defiance the laws of gravity and grammar.

—*The Atlantic Monthly*, 1892 on Emily Dickinson

164

If…it makes my body so cold no fire can warm me, I know that is poetry.

—Emily Dickinson

165

We take developmental psychology literally and blame our parents for everything we have become. The situation might change if we could see through those childhood stories, listen to them as myth, grasp their poetry, and hear the eternal mysteries singing through them.

—Thomas Moore

## 166

God is a comedian playing to an audience too afraid to laugh.

—Voltaire

## 167

Write films from your knowledge of life, not from your knowledge of films.

—Anonymous

## 168

A truly great book should be read in youth, again in maturity and once more in old age, as a fine building should be seen by morning light, at noon and by moonlight.

—Robertson Davies

## 169

Success is simply a matter of luck. Ask any failure.

—Earl Wilson

## 170

A true measure of your worth includes all the benefits others have gained from your successes.

—Cullen Hightower

## 171

The best time for planning a book is while you're doing the dishes.

—Agatha Christie

## 172

Through zeal, knowledge is gotten, through lack of zeal, knowledge is lost; let a man who knows this double path of gain and loss thus place himself that knowledge may grow.

—Buddha

## 173

One ought to write only when one leaves a piece of one's flesh in the inkpot each time one dips one's pen.

—Tolstoy

### 174

Too much research can be the disguise of procrastination or fear.

—Lew Hunter

### 175

Every man on the foundation of his own sufferings and joys, builds for all.

—Albert Camus

### 176

Character and thought are merely obscured by a diction that is over brilliant.

—Aristotle

### 177

Poets are the unacknowledged legislators of the world.

—Shelley

### 178

I like criticism, but it must be my way.

—Mark Twain

### 179

The charm, one might say the genius of memory, is that it is choosy, chancy and temperamental; it rejects the edifying cathedral and indelibly photographs the small boy outside, chewing a hunk of melon in the dust.

—Elizabeth Bowen

### 180

A man's work is his dilemma: his job is his bondage, but it also gives him a fair share of his identity and keeps him from being a bystander in somebody else's world.

—Melvin Maddocks

### 181

It takes twenty years to make an overnight success.

—Eddie Cantor

### 182

Do not take life too seriously. You will never get out alive.

—Elbert Hubbard

### 183

The most essential gift for a good writer is a built-in shock-proof shit detector. This is the writer's radar and all great writers have had it.

—Ernest Hemingway

### 184

The world of the living contains enough marvels and mysteries as it is—marvels and mysteries acting upon our emotions and intelligence in ways so inexplicable that it would almost justify the conception of life as an enchanted state.

—Joseph Conrad

### 185

Let your tears come. Let them water your soul.

—Eileen Mayhew

### 186

Speak when you are angry and you will make the best speech you will ever regret.

—Ambrose Bierce

### 187

Whatever people in general do not understand they are always prepared to dislike; the incomprehensible is always the obnoxious.

—Lettitia E. Landon

### 188

A different language is a different vision of life.

—Federico Fellini

### 189

The great men in literature have usually tried to bring the written word into harmony with the spoken, instead of encouraging an exclusive language to write in.

—John Erskine

190

Age is not a particularly interesting subject. Anyone can get old. All you have to do is live long enough.

—Groucho Marx

191

Which of us is not forever a stranger and alone?

—Virginia Wolfe

192

Experience is the name everyone gives to their mistakes.

—Oscar Wilde

193

The best work is done with the heart breaking, or overflowing.

—Mignon McLaughlin

194

Language is more fashion than science and matters of usage, spelling, and pronunciation tend to wander around like hemlines.

—Bill Bryson

195

My grandfather always said that life is like licking honey off a thorn.

—Louis Adamic

196

Do as much in dialog as you can as if it were in a play or in a movie.

—Sol Stein

197

If you can't annoy somebody, there is little point in writing.

—Kingsley Amis

### 198

Writing is turning one's worst moments into money.

—J.P. Donleavy

### 199

I couldn't wait for success, so I went ahead without it.

—Jonathan Winters

### 200

The world in general doesn't know what to make of originality; it is startled out of its comfortable habits of thought, and its first reaction is one of anger.

—W. Somerset Maugham

### 201

Why not spend time in determining what is worthwhile for us, and then go after that?

—William Ross

### 202

Better murder an infant in its cradle than nurse an unacted desire.

—William Blake

### 203

The truly creative mind in any field is no more than this: A human creature born abnormally, inhumanly sensitive. To him a touch is a blow, a sound is a noise, a misfortune is a tragedy, a joy is an ecstasy, a friend is a lover, a lover is a god, and failure is death. Add to this cruelly delicate organism the overpowering necessity to create, create, create—so that without the creating of music or poetry or books or buildings or something of meaning, his very breath is cut off from him. He must create, must pour out creation. By some strange, unknown, inward urgency he is not really alive unless he is creating.

—Pearl S. Buck

204

The next best thing to knowing something is knowing where to find it.

—Samuel Johnson

205

The end is the chief thing of all.

—Aristotle

206

I want you to spread your story and your characters before you as if you were to lift your intestines from your stomach and arrange them on a table. *Your* guts, not anyone else's. Get inside of yourself. Pull things out. Don't be safe.

—Lew Hunter

207

In every work of genius we recognize our own rejected thoughts.

—Ralph Waldo Emerson

208

Millions long for immortality who don't know what to do on a rainy Sunday afternoon.

—Susan Ertz

209

Those who write clearly have readers; those who write obscurely have commentators.

—Albert Camus

210

A word is not a crystal, transparent and unchanged, it is the skin of a living thought and may vary greatly in color and content according to the circumstances and time in which it is used.

—Oliver Wendell Holmes

211

Search your heart and soul for what you have to

contribute. Remember, your book must help someone with something.

—Cherie Carter-Scott

212

Nothing is so poor and melancholy as an art that is interested in itself and not its subject.

—George Santayana

213

He can compress the most words into the smallest idea of any man I ever met.

—Abraham Lincoln

214

What you notice depends on who you are.

—Douglas Adams

215

Be careful how you interpret the world: it "is" like that.

—Erich Heller

216

Do not commit the error, common among the young, of assuming that if you cannot save the whole of mankind, you have failed.

—Jan de Hartog

217

I am aware that no man is a villain in his own eyes.

—James Baldwin

218

There is no way out except through the last sentence.

—E.L. Doctorow

219

Money costs too much.

—Ross Macdonald

### 220

Only a mediocre person is always at his best.

—Somerset Maugham

### 221

The marvels—of film, radio, and television—are marvels of one-way communication, which is not communication at all.

—Milton Mayer

### 222

There is something that is much more scarce, something rarer than ability. It is the ability to recognize ability.

—Robert Half

### 223

Success is a journey, not a destination.

—Ben Sweetland

### 224

Nobody made you be a writer.

—William Goldman

### 225

There is an element of good fortune involved in getting your story to the right editor on the right day. Learn your market well, and accept that your odds are better here than in the lottery—but not by much.

—Catherine Ryan Hyde

### 226

Where the spirit does not work with the hand there is no art.

—Leonardo DaVinci

### 227

I love deadlines. I love the whooshing noise they make as they go by.

—Douglas Adams

### 228

Don't make an ideology out of your limitations.

—Tom Bourbon

### 229

Books had instant replay long before televised sports.

—Ben Williams

### 230

Beginners *Do* Break In Each Year.

—Jack M. Bickham

### 231

Writing *is* rewriting.

—Sol Stein

### 232

I think it is only a matter of time before you reach out into more substantial efforts that will be capable of making some real money as books.

—A rejection slip for James M. Cain's *The Postman Always Rings Twice*

### 233

The two most engaging powers of an author: new things are made familiar, familiar things are made new.

—Samuel Johnson

### 234

The most beautiful words in the English language are *Check Enclosed*.

—Dorothy Parker

### 235

If I am walking with two other men, each of them will serve as my teacher. I will pick out the good points of the one and imitate them and the bad points of the other and correct them in myself.

—Confucius

### 236

I became an artist when I stopped admiring and started remembering.

—Willa Cather

### 237

Until seventy, one learns wisdom, and then one goes and drops dead.

—Yiddish proverb

### 238

The cure for writer's cramp is writer's block.

—Inigo DeLeon

### 239

If the doctor told me I had only six minutes to live, I'd type a little faster.

—Isaac Asimov

### 240

A blank page is God's way of showing you how hard it is to be God.

—Anonymous

### 241

Never use a verb other than "said" to carry dialogue.

—Elmore Leonard

### 242

Do not believe that it is very much of an advance to do the unnecessary three times as fast.

—Peter Drucker

### 243

It is not interesting enough for the general reader and not thorough enough for the scientific reader.

—Rejection slip for H.G. Wells', *The Time Machine*

### 244

Nothing stinks like a pile of unpublished writing.

—Sylvia Plath

### 245

What a wonderful life I've had! I only wish I'd realized it sooner.

—Colette

### 246
The thoughtless are rarely wordless.

—Howard W. Newton

### 247
Mr. F. Scott Fitzgerald deserves a good shaking...*The Great Gatsby* is an absurd story, whether considered as romance, melodrama, or plain record of New York high life.

—Saturday Review of Literature

### 248
Who so has the power to affect us more and more deeply each time we read him is indeed a master, no matter what his name, rank or status be.

—Henry Miller

### 249
It is by the goodness of God that in our country we have those three unspeakably precious things: freedom of speech, freedom of conscience, and the prudence never to practice either of them.

—Mark Twain

### 250
Sometimes ideas are commercial because they are *good*.

—Greg Nava

### 251
In short, never put two people in the same scene who agree with each other.

—Lew Hunter

### 252
Melodrama is simply a story where guns are available to solve characters' problems.

—Lew Hunter

### 253
Act Three should be a happy or sad ending. Not

sort of happy or sort of sad, but extremely happy or extremely sad. One or the other.

—Lew Hunter

254

A man who is ill-adjusted to the world is always on the verge of finding himself. One who is adjusted to the world never finds himself, but gets to be a cabinet minister.

—Herman Hesse

255

When you watch television you never see people watching television. We love television because it brings us a world in which television does not exist.

—Barbara Ehrenreich

256

One of the first things schoolchildren in Texas learn is how to compose a simple declarative sentence without the word *shit* in it.

—Anonymous

257

Nobody made a greater mistake than he who did nothing because he could do only a little.

—Edmund Burke

258

You are never too old to be what you might have been.

—George Eliot

259

When nations grow old, the arts grow cold and commerce settles on every tree.

—William Blake

260

Though we travel the world over to find the beautiful, we must carry it with us or we find it not.

—Ralph Waldo Emerson

## 261

There are only two ways to live your life. One, as if nothing is a miracle, and the other as if everything is a miracle.

—Albert Einstein

## 262

The greatest foes, and whom we must chiefly combat, are within.

—Cervantes

## 263

If you would be a real seeker after truth, it is necessary that at least once in your life you doubt, as far as possible, all things.

—Rene Descartes

## 264

What we ever hope to do with ease, we must first learn to do with diligence.

—Samuel Johnson

## 265

Suffering is the sole origin of consciousness.

—Dostoyevsky

## 266

The only person you should ever compete with is yourself. You can't hope for a fairer match.

—Todd Ruthman

## 267

A story with a stupid central idea, no matter how brilliantly the story is told, will be a stupid story.

—John Gardner

## 268

Forget about the marketplace. Follow your obsession.

—Lew Hunter

### 269

Somewhere along the line we seem to have confused comfort with happiness.

—Dean Karnazes

### 270

Never mistake motion for action.

—Ernest Hemingway

### 271

You only live once, but if you work it right, once is enough.

—Joe Lewis

### 272

Success seems to be largely a matter of hanging on after others have let go.

—William Feather

### 273

In some circumstances, the refusal to be defeated is the refusal to be educated.

—Margaret Halsey

### 274

Humor is a way of saying something serious.

—T.S. Eliot

### 275

Man is bound to lie about himself.

—Dostoyevsky

### 276

Often the accurate answer to a usage question begins, "It depends". And what it depends on most often is where you are, who you are, who your listeners or readers are, and what your purpose in speaking or writing is.

—Kenneth G. Wilson

### 277

All slang is metaphor, and all metaphor is poetry.

—G.K. Chesterton

## 278

Write a nonfiction book and be prepared for the legion of readers who are going to doubt your fact. But write a novel, and get ready for the world to assume that every word is true.

—Barbara Kingsolver

## 279

The best writing has no lace on its sleeves.

—Walt Whitman

## 280

No man can be called friendless when he has God and the companionship of good books.

—Elizabeth Barret Browning

## 281

When you're a professional, you come back no matter what happened the day before.

—Billy Martin

## 282

Beauty and folly are generally companions.

—Balthasar Gracian

## 283

Tragedy is when I cut my finger. Comedy is when you walk into an open sewer and die.

—Mel Brooks

## 284

The joy about writing is that as long as you write from your heart, a thousand English degrees cannot compete with that.

—Fannie Flagg

## 285

Of his earlier poems, many are licentious; the later are chiefly devout. Few are good for much.

—Henry Hallam on John Donne

## 286

No man is an island, entire of itself; every man is a

piece of the continent, a part of the main.

—John Donne

287

Vocations which we wanted to pursue, but didn't, bleed like colors on the whole of our existence.

—Honore de Balzac

288

There are some who only employ words for the purpose of disguising their thoughts.

—Voltaire

289

If you see a man coming through a doorway, it means nothing. If you see him coming through a window, that is at once interesting.

—Billy Wilder

290

The success of the poem is determined not by how much the poet felt in writing it, but by how much the reader feels in reading it.

—John Ciardi

291

Anything written to please the author is worthless.

—Blaise Pascal

292

My purpose is to entertain myself first and other people secondly.

—John D. MacDonald

293

Tell the truth
But tell it slant.

—Emily Dickinson

294

Never give up and face the facts.

—Ruth Gordon

### 295

If I find 10,000 ways something doesn't work, I haven't failed.

—Thomas Edison

### 296

Words, too, are known by the company they keep.

—Josh Shipley

### 297

I'll rest when I'm dead.

—Warren Zevon

### 298

Anyone who stops learning is old, whether at twenty or eighty. Anyone who keeps learning stays young. The greatest thing in life is to keep your mind young.

—Henry Ford

### 299

The test of a real comedian is whether you laugh at him before he opens his mouth.

—George Jean Nathan

### 300

Unlike lawyers, engineers, teachers, physicians, and other more stable folk engaged in more common professional work, aspiring writers, when they envision success in their chosen field, presume that it will necessarily carry with it general fame and celebration.

—George V. Higgins

### 301

A closed mind is like a closed book: just a block of wood.

—Chinese proverb

### 302

Think not those faithful who praise all thy words and actions but those who kindly reprove thy faults.

—Socrates

### 303

A golden pen is no guarantee for good writing.

—Yiddish proverb

### 304

The writing of fiction is very deceptive. Like riding a bicycle, it looks easy until you try it. But whereas the bicycle gives you quick and painful proof that riding isn't quite as easy as it appeared, writing is more subtle; your very first story may look good to you—even though it's almost certainly unpublishable on later reflection.

—Jack M. Bickham

### 305

Literature is like any other trade; you will never sell anything unless you go to the right shop.

—George Bernard Shaw

### 306

If you find yourself taking out what you just put in, it's a sure sign the story is finished.

—Raymond Carver

### 307

The difference between false memories and true ones is the same as for jewels: it is always the false ones that look the most real, the most brilliant.

—Salvador Dali

### 308

It's great working for yourself but when you call in sick you know you're lying.

—Rita Rudner

### 309

Love yourself first and everything else falls into line.

—Lucille Ball

### 310

To the vast majority of mankind nothing is more agreeable than to escape the need for mental exertion....To most people nothing is more troublesome than the effort of thinking.

—James Bryce

### 311

Think wrongly, if you please, but in all cases think for yourself.

—Doris Lessing

### 312

If you refuse to accept anything but the very best, you very often get it.

—Somerset Maugham

### 313

Mistakes are part of the dues one pays for a full life.

—Sophia Loren

### 314

It is the essence of genius to make use of the simplest ideas.

—Charles Peguy

### 315

Poets are soldiers that liberate words from the steadfast possession of definition.

—Eli Kharmarov

### 316

Not being able to govern events, I govern myself.

—Michel De Montaigne

### 317

One should fight like the devil the temptation to think well of editors. They are all, without exception— at least some of the time—incompetent or crazy. By the nature of their profession they read too much, with the result they grow jaded and cannot recognize talent though it dances in front of their eyes.

—John Gardner

### 318

...too different from other juveniles on the market to warrant its selling.

—Rejection slip for Dr. Seuss' *And to Think I Saw it on Mulberry Street*

### 319

Comedy is the only business in the world where if you fuck up nobody laughs.

—Robin Williams

### 320

Life is like a game of cards. The hand that is dealt you represents determinism; the way you play it is free will.

—Jawaharlal Nehru

### 321

Language is the archives of history.

—Ralph Waldo Emerson

### 322

Man's mind stretched to a new idea never goes back to its original dimensions.

—Oliver Wendell Holmes

### 323

Words so innocent and powerless as they are standing in a dictionary, how potent for good and evil they become in the hands of one who knows how to combine them.

—Nathaniel Hawthorne

### 324

Genius is eternal patience.

—Michelangelo

### 325

Words are a commodity in which there is never any slump.

—Christopher Morley

## 326

Don't tell me the moon is shining, show me the glint of light on broken glass.

—Anton Chekhov

## 327

A crowded elevator smells different to a midget.

—Steve Sabol

## 328

Who will tell whether one happy moment of love or the joy of breathing or walking on a bright morning and smelling the fresh air, is not worth all the suffering and effort which life implies.

—Erich Fromm

## 329

The closest to perfection a person ever comes is when he fills out a job application.

—Stanley J. Randall

## 330

To me, it seems a dreadful indignity to have a soul controlled by geography.

—George Santayana

## 331

Every man of genius is considerably helped by being dead.

—Robert S. Lynd

## 332

I think in terms of the day's resolutions, not the year's.

—Henry Moore

## 333

One's real life is so often the life that one does not lead.

—Oscar Wilde

**334**

We can escape from the level of society, but not from the level of intelligence to which we are born.

—Randall Jarrell

**335**

A problem well stated is a problem half solved.

—Charles F. Kettering

**336**

A man has to live with himself, and he should see to it he always has good company.

—Charles Evans Hughes

**337**

Whatever has been well said by anybody is mine.

—Seneca

**338**

Much learning does not teach a man to have intelligence.

—Heraclitus

**339**

You're welcome to LeCarre—he hasn't got any future.

—Review of John LeCarre's *The Spy Who Came In From the Cold*

**340**

I find television very educating. Every time someone turns on the set I go into the other room and read a book.

—Groucho Marx

**341**

I'm always amazed at young writers, or arriving writers of any age, at how difficult it is to explain to them that they have so many stories right in their hands, locked in their lives, in their relationships, maybe in their awful jobs—it's not on the Siberian frontier.

—Thomas McGuane

### 342

If everybody waited until he or she had all available information before acting, we would make far fewer errors, but we'd never get anything done.

—Marilyn vos Savant

### 343

By words the mind is winged.

—Aristophanes

### 344

The world is a skirt I want to lift up.

—Hanif Kureishi

### 345

Do not let your peace depend on the hearts of others; whatever they say about you, good or bad, you are not because of it another, for you are as you are.

—Thomas a Kempis

### 346

The average critic never recognizes an achievement when it happens. He explains it after it has become respectable.

—Raymond Chandler

### 347

One word becomes a herd.

—Yiddish proverb

### 348

Be ashamed to die until you have won some victory for humanity.

—Horace Mann

### 349

Words are chameleons which reflect the color of their environment.

—Learned Hand

### 350

Hold yourself to a higher standard. Make each

article, poem, or book better than the last one. Your best writing could change someone's life.

—Lyndon Felt

351

The rules for writing a best-seller are simple:
—Take an idea you really like.
—Develop it until it is brilliant.
—Rewrite it for a year or two, until every word shines. Then bite your nails, hold your breath, and pray like mad.

—Sidney Sheldon

352

In Ireland, a writer is looked upon as a failed conversationalist.

—Anonymous

353

When I was young, I admired clever people. Now that I'm old, I admire kind people.

—Abraham Joshua Heschel

354

The world is round and the place which may seem like the end may also be only the beginning.

—George Baker

355

The whole problem with the world is that fools and fanatics are always so certain of themselves, and wiser people so full of doubts.

—Bertrand Russell

356

We should have a great many fewer disputes in the world if words were taken for what they are, the signs of our ideas, and not the things themselves.

—John Locke

357

The only person who can decide when the game is over and the writer has lost is the writer himself. When you think about it, that figures: he is the only person responsible for the decision to play it in the first place. If he did not win, well, most do not, and it is no disgrace.

—George V. Higgins

358

Some part of a mistake is always correct.

—Savielly Tartakower

359

One of the indictments of civilization is that happiness and intelligence are so rarely found in the same person.

—William Faulkner

360

Only dead fish swim with the stream.

—Anonymous

361

As a novelist, I tell people stories, and people give me money. Then financial planners tell me stories and I give them money.

—Martin Cruz Smith

362

My biggest piece of advice is don't use desperately boring description to elaborate on something technical or dole out heavy explanation for nothing detail. The reader will ignore it and be bored.

—Clive Cussler

363

I don't make jokes. I just watch the government and report the facts.

—Will Rogers

364

I write as a sow pisses.

—Mozart

### 365

An idealist is one who, on noticing that a rose smells better than a cabbage, concludes that it will also make better soup.

—H.L. Mencken

### 366

It is his life work to announce the obvious in terms of the scandalous.

—H.L. Mencken on George Bernard Shaw

### 367

Life does not cease to be funny when people die, any more than it ceases to be serious when people laugh.

—George Bernard Shaw

### 368

The mass of men lead lives of quiet desperation.

—Thoreau

### 369

A word after a word after a word is power.

—Margaret Atwood

### 370

Genuine poetry can communicate before it is understood.

—T.S. Eliot

### 371

The more we learn about this particular universe we live in, the more impossibly improbable it seems that we are here at all.

—Chet Raymo

### 372

We work to become, not to acquire.

—Elbert Hubbard

### 373

We can destroy ourselves by cynicism and disillusion just as effectively as by bombs.

—Kenneth Clark

## 374

Writing is a business, too. Aspiring authors—and those anxious to make it to the next plateau—require a business plan. Perhaps not as formal as the entrepreneur's, but just as realistic and objective....How long will it take? How much trouble will it be?

—Gene Perret

## 375

The most insipid, ridiculous play that I ever saw in my life.

—Samuel Pepys on Shakespeare's *A Midsummer Night's Dream*

## 376

Our dreams are the stuff that life is made of.

—William Shakespeare

## 377

At 18 our convictions are hills from which we look; at 45 they are caves in which we hide.

—F. Scott Fitzgerald

## 378

A hundred years from now it is very likely that *The Jumping Frog* alone will be remembered.

—Harry Thurston Peck on Mark Twain

## 379

The time to begin writing an article is when you have finished it to your satisfaction. By that time you begin to clearly and logically perceive what it is that you really want to say.

—Mark Twain

## 380

If we encounter a man of rare intellect, we should ask him what books he reads.

—Ralph Waldo Emerson

### 381

Read over your compositions and, when you meet a passage you think is particularly fine, strike it out.

—Samuel Johnson

### 382

He who dares not offend cannot be honest.

—Thomas Paine

### 383

If the English language made any sense a catastrophe would be an apostrophe with fur.

—Doug Larsen

### 384

Comedy is tragedy plus time.

—Woody Allen

### 385

Clarity is tragedy plus time.

—Jeff Lipsky

### 386

We are never more discontented with others than when we are discontented with ourselves.

—Henri Frederic Amiel

### 387

I met not long ago, a young man who aspired to become a novelist. Knowing that I was in the profession, he asked me to tell him how he should set to work to realize his ambition. I did my best to explain. 'The first thing,' I said, 'is to buy quite a lot of paper, a bottle of ink, and a pen. After that you merely have to write.'

—Aldous Huxley

### 388

Have patience! In time even grass becomes milk.

—Charan Singh

### 389

That had what I really like in a story. An ending.

—Homer Simpson

390

Be obscure clearly.

—E.B. White

391

But that is the humorist's goal in life—to have a comment ready on practically anything.

—Gene Perret

392

A pun is the lowest form of humor when you don't think of it first.

—Oscar Levant

393

No one is born a pro.

—Donald Westlake

394

Effort in one direction is always paid for as lost effort in another direction.

—Richard Dawkins

395

The more options you have to choose from in your writing, the better your writing will be.

—Gene Peret

396

If writers were good businessmen, they'd have too much sense to be writers.

—Irwin S. Cobb

397

What kind of writing pays the best?
Ransom notes.

—Lyndon Felt

398

Creative activity could be described as a type of learning process where teacher and pupil are located in the same individual.

—Arthur Koestler

### 399

The greatest masterpiece in literature is only a dictionary out of order.

—Jean Cocteau

### 400

There is no security on this earth; there is only opportunity.

—Douglas MacArthur

### 401

Learn to get in touch with that silence within yourself and know that everything in this life has a purpose.

—Elisabeth Kubler-Ross

### 402

Knowledge without experience is worse than useless.

—Anonymous

### 403

Study the craft of writing, but don't allow the *study* to replace your daily *writing*.

—Lyndon Felt

### 404

Words are like money, there is nothing so useless, unless when in actual use.

—Samuel Butler

### 405

Interpretation is the revenge of the intellect upon art.

—Susan Sontag

### 406

The ultimate creative capacity of the brain may be, for all practical purposes, infinite.

—George Leonard

### 407

Think with the whole body.

—Taisen Deshimaru

### 408

Don't ever be afraid to be wrong; this fear will hold back your intellectual development.

—Marilyn vos Savant

### 409

Attention is, in fact, a highly directed process. Shift the focus of attention, the area of interest, and totally new sensory data flow in.

—Richard Restak

### 410

Reality is merely an illusion, albeit a very persistent one.

—Albert Einstein

### 411

But as writers know, intense discomfort often helps to induce intensive work.

—Paul Bowles

### 412

From a certain point onward there is no longer any turning back. That is the point that must be reached.

—Franz Kafka.

### 413

No author is a man of genius to his publisher.

—Heinrich Heine

### 414

Life happens too fast for you ever to think about it. If you could just persuade people of this, but they insist on amassing education.

—Kurt Vonnegut, Jr.

### 415

Behind the phony tinsel of Hollywood lies the real tinsel.

—Oscar Levant

### 416

All life is a battlefield; whether we like it or not, we are born to fight. We have no choice in this but we do have the choice of our opponent and our weapon. If we fight other people we cannot but lose, but if we choose to fight all that is selfish and violent in us, we cannot but win.

—Eknath Easwaran

### 417

The day of the printed word is far from ended...the task of adding meaning and clarity remains urgent. People can not and need not absorb meaning at the speed of light.

—Erwin Canham

### 418

Words are of course the most powerful drug used by mankind.

—Rudyard Kipling

### 419

The cost of a thing is the amount of what I call life which is required to be exchanged for it immediately or in the long run.

—Thoreau

### 420

You can be sincere and still be stupid.

—Charles F. Kettering

### 421

If you aren't up to a little magic occasionally, maybe you shouldn't try writing.

—Lyndon Felt

### 422

I live on good soup, not fine words.

—Moliere

### 423

Deadlines clarify the mind.

—Thomas Blanton

### 424

The only effort worth making is the one it takes to learn the geography of one's own nature.

—Paul Bowles

### 425

Most bloggers have the private purpose of expressing themselves, for their own satisfaction. There is nothing wrong with that, but nothing demanding or especially admirable either.

—George Will

### 426

I think if you write something, you should publish it.

—Paul Bowles

### 427

Reality is a collective hunch.

—Lily Tomlin

### 428

It is such a fine line between stupid and clever.

—David St. Hubbins

### 429

History doesn't repeat itself; people do.

—Voltaire

### 430

Language is fossil poetry.

—Ralph Waldo Emerson

### 431

News is what people want to keep hidden. Everything else is publicity.

—Bill Moyers

### 432

I think the next best thing to solving a problem is finding some humor in it.

—Frank A. Clark

### 433
Discontent is the first step in the progress of a man or a nation.

—Oscar Wilde

### 434
Don't ever put your faith in what is changing; it has to fail you in time.

—Buddha

### 435
Nobody ever got started on a career as a writer by exercising good judgment, and no one ever will, either, so the sooner you break the habit of relying on yours the faster you will advance.

—George V. Higgins

### 436
We have read your manuscript with boundless delight. If we were to publish your paper, it would be impossible for us to publish any work of lower standard. And as it is unthinkable that in the next thousand years we shall see its equal, we are, to our regret, compelled to return your divine composition, and beg you a thousand times to overlook our short sight and timidity.

—Rejection slip from a Chinese publisher

### 437
Writing is, I suppose, a superstitious way of keeping the horror at bay, of keeping the evil outside.

—Paul Bowles

### 438
*Dictionary*, n. A malevolent literary device for cramping the growth of a language and making it hard and inelastic.

—Ambrose Bierce, from *The Devil's Dictionary*

### 439
You have reached the pinnacle of success as soon as you become uninterested in money,

compliments, or publicity.

—Thomas Wolfe

440

Watch what people are cynical about, and one can often discover what they lack.

—Harry Emerson Fosdick

441

Man's main concern is not to gain pleasure or to avoid pain but rather to see a meaning in life.

—Victor Frankl

442

If you don't believe that writing is the most important thing you can do with your life, save yourself the grief and give up now. Writing is too important to shirk and too difficult to simply dabble in.

—Lyndon Felt

443

Good people are good because they've come to wisdom through failure.

—William Saroyan

444

Every rejection slip is a step in the right direction.

—Ed Davis

445

It is as easy to dream a book as it is hard to write one.

—Honore de Balzac

446

The man who does not read good books has no advantage over the man that can't read them.

—Mark Twain

447

Queer—the rhymes were all wrong....They are quite as remarkable for defects as for beauties and are generally devoid of true poetical qualities.

—Rejection slip for Emily Dickinson's untitled manuscript

448

Don't hug fad-words without your fingers crossed.

—William Noble

449

I believe unhappiness should be studied very carefully; this is certainly no time for anyone to pretend to be happy, or to put his unhappiness away in the dark. (And anyone who is not unhappy now must be a monster, a saint, or an idiot.) You must watch your universe as it cracks above your head.

—Paul Bowles

450

You become a writer by writing.

—R.K. Narayan

451

As repressed sadists are supposed to become policemen or butchers, so those with irrational fear of life become publishers.

—Cyril Connolly

452

To use many words to communicate few thoughts is everywhere the unmistakable sign of mediocrity. To gather much thought into few words stamps the man of genius.

—Arthur Schopenhauer

453

The more words, the less wisdom.

—Anonymous

454

Words make another place, a place to escape to with your spirit alone.

—Robert MacNeil

## 455

Words ought to be a little wild for they are the assault of thoughts on the unthinking.

—John Maynard Keynes

## 456

The great enemy of clear language is insincerity. When there is a gap between one's real and one's declared aims, one turns, as it were instinctively to long words and exhausted idioms...

—George Orwell

## 457

Don't go into great detail describing places and things.

—Elmore Leonard

## 458

Work is an extension of personality. It is achievement. It is one of the ways in which a person defines himself, measures his worth, and his humanity.

—Peter F. Drucker

## 459

Always remember, individualism is what makes screenplays great, not their uniqueness.

—Lew Hunter

## 460

No time to write today? Set an egg timer for three minutes. Sit at the keyboard and write a three minute mystery: beginning, middle, and end. Even if you only do ten push-ups a day you'll be stronger at the end of a year.

—Lyndon Felt

## 461

I'm not the young writer of promise anymore. I'm an overworked claim.

—John Steinbeck

### 462

Books are companions, teachers, magicians, bankers of the treasures of the mind…humanity in print.

—Barbara W. Tuchman

### 463

The people who read me can get off the subway and go home feeling better about their own crappy lives, and luckier than the people they've been reading about.

—Jacqueline Susann

### 464

Anyone can write a novel given six weeks, pen, paper and no telephone or wife.

—Evelyn Waugh

### 465

When it comes right down to it, nothing has changed. The English sentence is as difficult to write as it ever was.

—John Steinbeck

### 466

For every flowering thought there will be a page like a wet and mangy mongrel…for every looping flight, a tap on the wing and a reminder that wax cannot hold the feathers firm too near the sun.

—John Steinbeck

### 467

I use those long, dull openings to weed out the ribbon clerks.

—James A. Michener

### 468

Writing can only be done because you go into a kind of euphoria—your child is beautiful no matter how ugly.

—Christopher Lehmann-Haupt

### 469

Literature is mostly about having sex and not much about having children; life is the other way around.

—David Lodge

### 470

I work so slowly that I could write in my own blood without hurting myself.

—Fran Lebowitz

### 471

When I say "work" I only mean writing. Everything else is odd jobs.

—Margaret Laurence

### 472

Writers have a rare power not given to anyone else; we can bore people long after we are dead.

—Sinclair Lewis

### 473

When a man publishes a book, there are so many stupid things said that he declares he'll never do it again. The praise is almost always worse than the criticism.

—Sherwood Anderson

### 474

I have long felt that any reviewer who expresses rage and loathing for a novel is preposterous. He or she is like a person who has just put on full armor and attacked a hot fudge sundae or banana split.

—Kurt Vonnegut

### 475

It's surprising that authors should expect kindness to be shown to their books when they are not themselves known for kindness toward their characters, their culture or by implication their readers.

—Anatole Broyard

### 476

A person who publishes a book willfully appears before the populace with his pants down...If it is a good book nothing can hurt him. If it is a bad book, nothing can help him.

—Edna St. Vincent Millay

477

Fiction reveals truths that reality obscures.

—Jessamyn West

478

Style is not a seductive decoration added to functional structure; it is the essence of a work of art.

—Evelyn Waugh

479

There is nothing to be gained...looking for certain patterns where none exist. Every life is full of pieces that do not fit.

—Michael Sheldon

480

A unanimous chorus of approval is not an assurance of survival; authors who please everyone at once are quickly exhausted.

—Andre Gide

481

Reviewers do not read books with much care. Their profession is more given to stupidity and malice and literary ignorance even than the professional novelist.

—Anthony Burgess

482

The only books that influence us are those for which we are ready, and which have gone a little farther down our particular path than we have got ourselves.

—E.M. Forster

483

First you have the writer who can write but can't spell. Then you have the editor who can spell but can't write. Finally you have the publisher who can neither spell nor write, and he makes all the money.

—Anonymous

Some reviews give pain. This is regrettable, but no author has the right to whine. He was not obliged to be an author. He invited publicity, and he must take the publicity that comes along.

—E.M. Forster

485

It is advantageous to an author that his book should be attacked as well as praised. Fame is a shuttlecock. If it be struck at one end of the room, it will soon fall to the ground. To keep it up, it must be struck at both ends.

—Samuel Johnson

486

Nature fits all her children with something to do, He who would write and can't write, can surely review.

—James Russell Lowell

487

Critics are like eunuchs in a harem. They're there every night, they see it done every night, they see how it should be done every night, but they can't do it themselves.

—Brendan Behan

488

It has sometimes occurred to me that the literary world would be much improved if critics just wrote the literature in the first place, thus avoiding that roundabout process in which the author struggles inside the complex of his book, like Laocoon contending with myriad problems, while the critic whisks through the finished book in a few minutes and immediately spots the gross blunders the author has taken over a year or more to make.

—William Stafford

### 489

I've probably missed some good reviews of my work over the years, but never a bad one—some fellow author is always eager to tell me about the bad ones.

—Edward Abbey

### 490

I do not believe writers should read reviews of their own books, and I do not. If one is not careful one is soon writing to please the reviewers and not their audience or themselves.

—Louis L'Amour

### 491

The only abnormality is the incapacity to love.

—Anais Nin

### 492

You wouldn't say an ax handle has style to it. It has beauty, and appropriateness of form and a "this-is-how-it-should-be-ness." But it has no style because it has no mistakes. Style reflects one's idiosyncrasies. Your personality is apt to show more to the degree that you did not solve the problem than to the degree you did.

—Charles Eames

### 493

Poetry is going on all the time in my head and I occasionally snip off a length.

—John Ashberry

### 494

I was writing stories when I was five…don't know what I did before that. Just loafed I suppose.

—P.G. Wodehouse

### 495

Lost years are worse than lost money.

—Yiddish proverb

### 496

The longer I live the more beautiful life becomes.

—Frank Lloyd Wright

### 497

No one can write decently who is distrustful of the reader's intelligence, or whose attitude is patronizing.

—E.B. White

### 498

Whitman is as unacquainted with art as a hog is with mathematics.

—A reviewer on Walt Whitman

### 499

To have great poetry there must be great audiences, too.

—Walt Whitman

### 500

Don't get cute with spellings and dialogue.

—William Noble

### 501

And still on the subject of books: Our daily news sources, newspapers and TV, are now so craven, so unvigilant on behalf of the American people, so uninformative, that only in  books do we learn what's really learn what's going on.

—Kurt Vonnegut

### 502

There is only one success—to be able to spend your life in your own way.

—Christopher Marley

### 503

This is your writing career.  You have to take control of it.  It doesn't belong to the other writers you know, nor to the editors, publishers or producers that you deal with.  It's yours.

—Gene Perret

### 504

There are only three rules that govern the composition of a novel.  Unfortunately no one knows what they are.

—Thornton Wilder

### 505

Reason often makes mistakes, but conscience never does.

—Josh Billings

### 506

Things are not what they seem to be: nor are they otherwise.

—The Lankavatra Sutra

### 507

Everybody's talking about people breaking into houses but there are more people in the world who want to break out of houses.

—Thornton Wilder

### 508

Time has no divisions to mark its passing.  There is never a thunderstorm to announce the beginning of a new month or year.

—Thomas Mann

### 509

Never use the words "suddenly" or "all hell broke loose."

—Elmore Leonard

### 510

It has not been for nothing that the word has remained man's principal toy and tool: without the meanings and values it sustains, all man's other tools would be worthless.

—Lewis Mumford

### 511

The words in prose ought to express the intended meaning, and no more; if they attract attention to themselves, it is, in general, a fault.

—Samuel Taylor Coleridge

### 512

How often we recall, with regret, that Napoleon once shot at a magazine editor and missed him and killed a publisher. But we remember, with charity, that his intentions were good.

—Mark Twain

### 513

The advertisements in a newspaper are more full of knowledge in respect to what is going on in a state or community than the editorial columns are.

—Henry Ward Beecher

### 514

When I was a child I thought being a writer would be fun and easy. By "child" I mean my twenties and thirties.

—Beth Greene

### 515

Isn't egomania always the precondition of all creative work? I have found little to dispel that notion.

—Tennessee Williams

### 516

Your boasting will mean that you have failed.

—Lao-Tzu

### 517

Success is enduring failure after failure with no loss of enthusiasm.

—Anonymous

### 518

Any time you're in the presence of greatness—even if it's a presence once or twice removed—a little bit of it rubs off on you. Not the skills, necessarily, but the energy. It can inspire you to attack your own work with more gusto. That renewed vigor can improve your skills.

—Gene Perret

519

No one can make you feel inferior without your own consent.

—Eleanor Roosevelt

520

Interest in Alaska has subsided to an amazing degree. Then, again, so much has been written, that I do not think it would pay to buy your story.

—*The San Francisco Bulletin's* rejection slip for Jack London's Yukon stories.

521

The proper function of man is to live, not exist.
I shall not waste my days in trying to prolong them.
I shall use my time.

—Jack London

522

Without knowing the force of words, it is impossible to know men.

—Confucius

523

When ideas fail, words come in very handy.

—Goethe

524

You can learn little from victory. You can learn everything from defeat.

—Christy Mathewson

525

The good writer seems to be writing about himself, but has his eye always on that thread of the Universe which runs through himself and all things.

—Ralph Waldo Emerson

### 526

Take pride in those rejection slips; it means that you are in the game and playing.

—Lyndon Felt

### 527

Books are a narcotic.

—Franz Kafka

### 528

Books worth reading are worth re-reading.

—Holbrook Jackson

### 529

You can't tell a book by its movie.

—Louis A. Safian

### 530

Most books are propaganda, direct or indirect.

—George Orwell

### 531

The oldest books are only just out to those who have not read them.

—Samuel Butler

### 532

The easiest books are generally the best, for whatever author is obscure and difficult in his own language certainly does not think clearly.

—Lord Chesterfield

### 533

One always tends to overpraise a long book, because one has got through it.

—E.M. Forster

### 534

The best service a book can render you is not to impart truth, but to make you think it out for yourself.

—Elbert Hubbard

### 535

Hope is independent of the apparatus of logic.

—Norman Cousins

### 536

Standard English is a convenient abstraction, like the average man.

—George Leslie Brook

### 537

Writing became a struggle to create completely fresh forms out of rocks and sticks of words...to see things for the first time...to find the extraordinary behind the ordinary.

—Patrick White

### 538

Delay is natural to a writer. He is like a surfer—he bides his time, waits for the perfect wave on which to ride in...for the surge (of emotion? Of strength? Of courage?) that will carry him along.

—E.B. White

### 539

Good communication is as stimulating as black coffee, and just as hard to sleep after.

—Anne Morrow Lindberg

### 540

Nothing comes easy.

—Yiddish proverb

### 541

But there was something even worse and something that must be avoided at all costs: if the words and the sentiments were dishonest, the author was faking it, writing about things he didn't care about or believe in, then nobody could ever care anything about it.

—Raymond Carver

### 542

Follow your bliss.

—Joseph Campbell

### 543
The books that the world calls immoral are books that show the world its own shame.
—Oscar Wilde

### 544
*Classic*: A book which people praise and don't read.
—Mark Twain

### 545
Books are good enough in their own way, but they are a mighty bloodless substitute for life.
—Robert Louis Stevenson

### 546
A book is a mirror: if an ape look into it, an apostle is unlikely to look out.
—Georg Christoph Lichetenberg

### 547
Ideas brush past fleeting and insubstantial as moths. But I let them go, I don't want them. What I want is a voice.
—Joyce Carol Oates

### 548
The heart that breaks open can contain the entire universe.
—Joan Macy

### 549
The foolish and the dead alone never change their attitude.
—James Russell Lowell

### 550
One of the greatest labor-saving inventions of today is tomorrow.
—Vincent T. Foss

### 551
When you lose, don't lose the lesson.
—Anonymous

552

A poem begins with a lump in the throat.

—Robert Frost

553

I lie awake and think about the past.

—Ronald Knox

554

All of us have much to learn about our craft. We can learn it from the masters, from the editors and publishers, and from our fellow writers.

—Gene Perret

555

We are not interested in science fiction which deals with negative utopias. They don't sell.

—One of Stephen King's early rejections

556

Only enemies speak the truth; friends and lovers lie endlessly, caught in the web of duty.

—Stephen King

557

The writer is an explorer. Every step is an advance into new land.

—Ralph Waldo Emerson

558

You can discover more about a person in an hour of play than in a year of discussion.

—Plato

559

It is with words as with sunbeams, the more they are condensed, the deeper they burn.

—Robert Souther

560

If you tell the truth you don't have to swear.

—Yiddish proverb

### 561

*Wit*, n, The salt with which the American humorist spoils his intellectual cookery by leaving it out.

—Ambrose Bierce, from *The Devil's Dictionary*

### 562

Journalism is literature in a hurry.

—Matthew Arnold

### 563

That is what we are supposed to do when we are at our best—make it all up—but make it up so truly that later it will happen just that way.

—Ernest Hemingway

### 564

How can you write if you can't cry?

—Ring Lardner

### 565

The future exists first in imagination, then in will, then in reality.

—Barbara Marx Hubbard

### 566

The best work is done with the heart breaking, or overflowing.

—Mignon McLaughlin

### 567

Most advice sucks.

—Lyndon Felt

### 568

The creative process takes its own course. If it did otherwise it would not be creative.

—F.W. Martin

### 569

To be fertile in hypotheses is the first requisite of creativity, and to be willing to throw them away the moment experience contradicts them is the next.

—William James

### 570

Discontent is at the root of the creative process.

—Eric Hoffer

### 571

Proximity to the crowd, to the majority view, spells the death of creativity. For a soul can create only when alone, and some are chosen for the flowering that takes place in the dark avenues of the night.

—Abraham Joshua Heschel

### 572

Beware the man of one book.

—Italian saying

### 573

If you want to get across an idea, wrap it up as a person

—Ralph J. Bunche

### 574

Every new idea has something of the pain and peril of childbirth about it.

—Samuel Butler

### 575

There is no such thing as writer's block—writers write; it's that simple.

—George V. Higgins

### 576

When a thing has been said and well said, have no scruple; take it and copy it.

—Anatole France

### 577

His style has the desperate jauntiness of an orchestra fiddling away for dear life on a sinking ship.

—Edmund Wilson, on Evelyn Waugh

### 578

We cherish our friends not for their ability to amuse us, but for ours to amuse them.

—Evelyn Waugh

### 579

Education begins by teaching children to read and ends by making most of them hate reading.

—Holbrook Jackson

### 580

An editor is a person who knows more about writing than writers do but who has escaped the terrible desire to write.

—E.B. White

### 581

Writing is adding; editing is subtracting.

—E.B. White

### 582

The main failure of education is that it has not prepared people to comprehend matters concerning human destiny.

—Norman Cousins

### 583

Most editors are failed writers—but so are most writers.

—T.S. Eliot

### 584

*Editor.* A person employed on a newspaper, whose business it is to separate the wheat from the chaff, and to see that the chaff is printed.

—Elbert Hubbard

### 585

The freedom to make mistakes provides the best environment for creativity.

—Anonymous

### 586

Periods of tranquility are seldom prolific of creative achievement. Mankind has to be stirred up.

—Alfred North Whitehead

### 587

Mentally, fallow is as important as seedtime.  Even bodies can be exhausted by over cultivation.

—George Bernard Shaw

### 588

The motive force which impels a man or woman to embark upon the hazardous, often unrewarding task of endeavoring to make coherence out of the external world or out of their own inner selves often originates from alienation and despair.

—Anthony Storr

### 589

One must have chaos in one, to give birth to a dancing star.

—Friedrich Nietzsche

### 590

Freedom is nothing but a chance to be better.

—Albert Camus

### 591

The tragedies of maturer life cannot surpass the first tragedies of youth.

—Mark Twain

### 592

The scribbler's obligation when writing about characters whose conduct is comical is precisely the same as his obligation when writing about characters whose behavior is reprehensible: present the data without authorial comment, and have the decency to allow the reader to interpret the facts for himself.

—George V. Higgins

### 593

I don't understand the creative process.  Actually, I make more than a concerted effort *not* to understand it. I don't know what it is or how it works but I am *terrified* that one green morning it will decide to not work anymore, so I have always given it as wide a bypass as possible.

—William Goldman

594

Where you stumble there lies your treasure.

—Joseph Campbell

595

I am a part of all I have read.

—John Kieran

596

I shall tell you a great secret, my friend. Do not wait for the last judgment, it takes place every day.

—Albert Camus

597

Dying in vain isn't really all that bad since nearly everyone does it. It's the living in vain you really have to watch out for.

—Ross Thomas

598

The writing of dialog really cannot be learned and cannot be taught. You either have the gift or you don't. If you have the gift, you can refine it and improve on it and learn to handle it, but the absence of it is like tone deafness or the inability to imitate people.

—John O'Hara

599

Of course weather is necessary to a narrative of human experience. That is conceded. But it ought to be put where it will not be in the way; where it will not interrupt the flow of the narrative.

—Mark Twain.

600

Don't be afraid to say *Said*.

—Jack M. Bickham

### 601

Reading is to the mind what exercise is to the body.

—Sir Richard Steele

### 602

*Sartor Resartus* is simply unreadable, and for me that always sort of spoils a book.

—Will Cuppy on Thomas Carlyle's *Sartor Resartus*

### 603

A man lives by believing something, not by debating and arguing about many things.

—Thomas Carlyle

### 604

I cannot write any sort of story unless there is at least one character for whom I have a physical attraction.

—Tennessee Williams

### 605

He believed in his power with that belief which *is* the power.

—John G. Neihardt

### 606

A writer has two loyalties…he belongs to the special tribe of writers…he also belongs to a culture, to his own country.

—Octavio Paz

### 607

Peace goes into the making of a poem as flour goes into the making of bread.

—Pablo Neruda

### 608

Anything can make us look, only art can make us see.

—Archibald MacLeish

### 609

A writer is a descendent of other writers.

—Octavio Paz

### 610

The thing that makes poetry different from all of the other arts is you're using language, which is what you use for everything else—telling lies and selling socks, advertising, and conducting law. Whereas we don't write little concerts or paint little pictures.

—W.S. Merwin

### 611

Omissions are not accidents.

—Marianne Moore

### 612

Novels are about other people and poems are about yourself.

—Philip Larkin

### 613

A poem is a sort of verbal device to preserve a feeling you have had, so anyone who inserts the penny of his attention will receive that emotion neatly wrapped.

—Philip Larkin

### 614

Journalism is concerned with events, poetry with feelings. Journalism is concerned with the look of the world, poetry with the feel of the world.

—Archibald MacLeish

### 615

A good poet is someone who manages, in a lifetime of standing out in thunderstorms, to be struck by lightening five or six times; a dozen or two dozen and he is great.

—Randall Jarrell

### 616

A true poet writes because he must, not because he hopes to make a living from his poems.

—Robert Graves

### 617

Poetry is the language in which man explores his own amazement.

—Christopher Fry

### 618

To be a poet is a condition, not a profession.

—Robert Frost

### 619

When you meet a master swordsman, show him your sword. When you meet a man who is not a poet, do not show him your poem.

—Lin-Chi

### 620

To read fast is as bad as to eat in a hurry.

—Vilhelm Ekland

### 621

I write because I want more than one life; I insist on a wider selection. It's greed, plain and simple.

—Anne Tyler

### 622

You cannot solve a problem with the same thinking that created it.

—Albert Einstein

### 623

It is not enough for a story to flow. It has to kind of trickle and glint as it crosses over the stones of bare facts.

—John Updike

### 624

The difference between travel writing and fiction is…between recording what the eye sees and discovering what the imagination knows.

—Paul Theroux

### 625

I don't believe the writer should know too much

where he is going....He runs into old man blueprint.

—James Thurber

626

When rewriting, pretend someone will give you $100 for every word you are able to cut.

—Noah Lukeman

627

A professional writer is an amateur who didn't quit.

—Richard Bach

628

The published authors that you idolize and respect began just like you:  An amateur with a dream and a blank sheet of paper.

—Lyndon Felt

629

Most good or even great conductors, composers, microbiologists, ballerinas, mathematicians, visual artists, astronomers, or fighter pilots learned their business from older and more accomplished practitioners.

—Raymond Carver

630

First perfect your instrument.  Then just play.

—Charlie Parker

631

They may forget what you said, but they will never forget how you made them feel.

—Carl Buechner

632

The writer attempts to bridge the world of childhood with words, knowing all the while that, should the wound heal, he would no longer be a writer.

—Richard Selzer

### 633

The things one says are all unsuccessful attempts to say something else.

—Bertrand Russell

### 634

One page a day. If I produce more, it is too much. Less, it is not enough.

—Philip Roth

### 635

Irony is the whiskey of the mind.

—J.B. Priestley

### 636

If you get the landscape right, the characters will step out of it, and they'll be in the right place.

—Anne Proulx

### 637

Sometimes ordinary speech is banal…but if selected with art…can reveal the inner life, often fantastic, concealed in the speaker.

—V.S. Pritchett

### 638

My senses bruise easily, and when they are bruised, I write.

—S.J. Perelman

### 639

The greatest service a novelist can do his fellow man is…to attack the fake in the name of the real.

—Walker Percy

### 640

Talented or gifted writers? We should talk of gifted and talented readers.

—Milorad Pavic

### 641

The first sentence of every novel should be: "Trust

me, this will take time but there is order here, very faint, very human." Meander if you want to get to town.

—Michael Ondaatje

642

Good prose is like a windowpane.

—George Orwell

643

Writing isn't an occupation, but a duty. I write as much to understand as to be understood.

—Elie Wiesel

644

The essayist is a self-liberated man, sustained by the childish belief that everything he thinks about, everything he thinks about, everything that happens to him, is of general interest.

—E.B. White

645

My own education operated by a succession of eye-openers each involving the repudiation of some previously held belief.

—George Bernard Shaw

646

There is only one right form for a story and if you fail to find that form the story will not tell itself.

—Mark Twain

647

Writing is, finally, the art and opportunity of making yourself and others feel alive.

—Lyndon Felt

648

If you're a writer, you want to get your soul out there, where people can look at it.

—Jeremy Larner

### 649

I see the past as my territory...a foreign correspondent who goes there instead of to India or South America.

—David McCullough

### 650

I am by profession a snoop; by craft, a writer; by trade, a gossip.

—Martin Mayer

### 651

One of my greatest pleasures in writing has come from the thought that perhaps my work might annoy someone of comfortably pretentious position. Then comes the saddening realization that such people rarely read.

—John Kenneth Galbraith

### 652

If one is to write, one must believe—in the truth and worth of the scrawl, in the ability of the reader to receive and decode the message. No one can write decently who is distrustful of the reader's intelligence, or whose attitude is patronizing.

—E.B. White

### 653

As it is my design to make those that can scarcely read understand, I shall therefore avoid every literary ornament and put it in language as plain as the alphabet.

—Thomas Paine

### 654

My life does not go well *without* writing. It is my flywheel...cloister...communication with myself and God...my eyes to the world...window for awareness, without which I cannot see anything or walk straight.

—Anne Morrow Lindbergh

### 655

I write because I have two daughters and they need high-heeled shoes!

—Naguib Mahfouz

### 656

You will write if you will write without thinking of the result in terms of a result, but think of the writing in terms of discovery, which is to say the creation must take place between the pen and the paper, not before in a thought or afterwards in a recasting. Yes, before in a thought, but not in careful thinking. It will come if it is there and if you will let it come.

—Gertrude Stein

### 657

The only place worth writing about is the human heart…that bleak and wonderful terrain…the principal responsibility of the novelist.

—James Michener

### 658

All novels are about certain minorities: the individual is a minority.

—Ralph Ellison

### 659

Some men take up with chorus girls. I wrote a novel instead.

—Umberto Eco

### 660

Writing arrives like the wind, naked, mere ink, writing, and it passes by like nothing else in life, nothing except life itself.

—Marguerite Dumas

### 661

We will be judged on the splendor of our failures.

—William Faulkner

### 662

I have no talent; it's a question of working, of being willing to put in the time.

—Graham Greene

### 663

Writing is a logical extension of the adolescent daydream…most clearly a way of making daily life into a wonderfully unusual thing instead of a grind.

—Shirley Jackson

### 664

It is the beginning of the end when you discover you have style.

—Dashiell Hammett

### 665

Stories only happen to the people who can tell them.

—Allan Gurganus

### 666

Nouns and verbs are the guts of the language. Beware of covering them up with adjectives and adverbs.

—A.E. Guthrie Jr.

### 667

Every creative writer worth our consideration is a victim: a man given over to an obsession.

—Graham Greene

### 668

The characters in my novels are an amalgam of bits of real people. Real people are too limiting.

—Graham Greene

### 669

Of course, you only live one life, and you make all your mistakes, and learn what not to do, and that's the end of you.

—Richard Feynman

### 670

Publicity is a whore.

—Abraham Pais

### 671

A writer's knowledge of himself, realistic and unromantic, is like a store of energy on which he must draw for a lifetime: one volt of it properly directed will bring a character alive.

—Graham Greene

### 672

When people are talking about what they love and what they fear, everybody's eloquent.

—Allan Gurganis

### 673

I wonder how all those who don't write, compose or paint, can manage to escape the madness, melancholia and panic which is inherent in the human situation.

—Graham Greene

### 674

A writer is selected by his subject—his subject being the consciousness of his own era.

—Nadine Gordimer

### 675

You can get help from teachers, but you are going to have to learn a lot by yourself, sitting alone in a room.

—Theodor Geisel

### 676

The characters that I create are parts of myself and I send them on little missions to find out what I don't know yet.

—Gail Godwin

### 677

My way of "possessing" the people I love is to immure them in a palace of sentences.

—Jean Genet

### 678

I was the first writer I ever met.

—Margaret Drabble

### 679

A writer who never explored words, never searched, seeded, sieved, sifted through his knowledge and memory: dictionaries, thesaurus, poems, favorite paragraphs, to find the right word, is like someone owning a gold mine who has never mined it.

—Rumer Godden

### 680

The personality of a writer does become important after we have read his book and began to study it, but study is only a serious form of gossip. It teaches us everything about the book except the central thing.

—E.M. Forster

### 681

The use of language is all we have to pit against death and silence.

—Joyce Carol Oates

### 682

People read novellas, but they tend to live in novels.

—Howard Nemero

### 683

In all art, about one tenth is skill and the rest is personality.

—Sean O'Faolain

### 684

A novel is the smallest number of characters in the least number of situations necessary to precipitate a given crisis.

—Frank O'Connor

### 685

An autobiography can distort but fiction never lies. It reveals the writer totally.

—V.S. Naipaul

### 686

I am the kind of writer that people think other people are reading.

—V.S. Naipaul

### 687

I don't talk about other writers' work because I don't know enough, and I am reluctant to talk about my own because I know too much.

—Flannery O'Connor

### 688

We die. That may be the meaning of life. But we do language. That may be the measure of our lives.

—Toni Morrison

### 689

The middle-aged vice of completeness and over comprehensiveness has taken the place of my youthful vice of sketchiness and superficiality.

—Lewis Mumford

### 690

The unconscious…that's where the gold is, if there is any gold…the big room…unknowable, and only intermittently can we go into it.

—Edna O'Brien

### 691

I have rewritten—often several times—every word I have ever published. My pencils outlast their erasers.

—Vladimir Nabokov

### 692

I don't like to answer questions in novels. I only like to ask them.

—Brian Moore

### 693

Be regular and orderly in your life so that you may be violent and original in your work.

—Gustave Flaubert

### 694

The problems of the human heart in conflict with itself...alone can make good writing because only that is worth writing about, worth the agony and the sweat.

—William Faulkner

### 695

A writer should never be brief at the expense of being clear.

—Arthur Schopenhauer

### 696

Writers should use common words to say uncommon things.

—Arthur Schopenhauer

### 697

He who writes carelessly confesses...that he does not attach much importance to his thoughts.

—Arthur Schopenhauer

### 698

Dislike, displeasure, resentment, fault-finding, imagination, passionate, remonstrance, a sense of injustice---they all make fine fuel. Life can't ever really defeat a writer who's in love with writing.

—Edna Ferber

### 699

Writing is not a profession but a vocation of unhappiness.

—Georges Simenon

### 700

A man may write at any time, if he will set himself doggedly to it.

—Samuel Johnson

## 701

Do not hoard what seems good for a later place in the book, or for another book, give it, give it all, give it now.

—Annie Dillard

## 702

As an author you can play all the parts, arrange the scenery, be the whole show and nobody gets in the way.

—Robertson Davies

## 703

Books aren't written, they're rewritten…one of the hardest things in the world to accept, especially after the seventh rewrite hasn't done it.

—Michael Creighton

## 704

Even poets cannot write their own life story. Too many true lies, too many tangles.

—Jean Cocteau

## 705

There's nothing immoral in my books, only murder.

—Agatha Christie

## 706

An author arrives at a good style when language performs what is required of it without shyness.

—Cyril Connolly

## 707

Better to write for yourself and have no public than to write for the public and have no self.

—Cyril Connolly

## 708

I have to find a way of saying the truth without saying it; that is exactly what is literature after all, clever lies which secretly say the truth.

—Simone DeBeauvoir

### 709

All writers are a little crazy, but if they are any good they have a kind of terrible honesty.

—Raymond Chandler

### 710

Technique alone is just an embroidered potholder.

—Raymond Chandler

### 711

The most durable thing in writing is style, and style is the most valuable investment a writer can make with his time.

—Raymond Chandler

### 712

The discipline of the writer is to be still and listen to what his subject has to tell him.

—Rachel Carson

### 713

Good writing is rewriting.

—Truman Capote

### 714

Finishing a book is just like you took a child out in the yard and shot it.

—Truman Capote

### 715

The fewer writers you know the better, and if you're working on anything, don't tell them.

—Maeve Brennan

### 716

The most important thing a writer can have is the ability to live with constant loneliness and a strong sense of revulsion for the banalities of everyday socializing.

—Hunter S. Thompson

### 717

Next to the doing of things that deserve to be written, there is nothing that gets a man more credit, or gives him more pleasure, than to write things that deserve to be read.

—Pliny the Younger

718

Being a writer in a library is rather like being a eunuch in a harem.

—John Braine

719

It can't be taught...the only thing you can do for someone who wants to write is to buy them a typewriter.

—James M. Cain

720

Every writer knows that he has just so many of these ova in his belly, and indeed he is never sure that the latest one he produced will not be his last.

—James M Cain

721

You have to know how to accept rejection and reject acceptance.

—Ray Bradbury

722

Characters are not created by writers. They pre-exist and have to be found.

—Elizabeth Bowen

723

Every writer has a family out there, a group of people who share his vision and his dream. If he persists, he will find them.

—Richard Bach

724

Writing is brain work, but there is something that feels to me like physiological involvement. A kind of contracting and relaxing moment going on in the front part of my head just behind the forehead as I write.

—Vance Bourjaly

### 725

Poetry is perfection's sweat but most seen as fresh as the raindrops on a statue's brow.

—Derek Walcott

### 726

The fate of poetry is to fall in love with the world, in spite of History.

—Derek Walcott

### 727

I am longing for censorship—because nobody better than censors understood all the subtle nuances of poetry. Nobody appreciated us so highly.

—Yevgeny Yevtushenko

### 728

A novel is never anything but a philosophy put into images.

—Albert Camus

### 729

Of all escape mechanisms, death is the most effective.

—H.L. Mencken

### 730

One of the functions of intelligence is to take account of the dangers that from trusting solely to the intelligence.

—Lewis Mumford

### 731

Don't go to a pine cabin all alone and brood and write. You reach that stage soon enough anyway.

—Truman Capote

### 732

The work itself is hard and slow, and the writer's illumination becomes a taskmaster, a ruling discipline, jealously guarding the mind until the book is done.

—E.L. Doctorow

### 733

It's my experience that if I write too much in one day, it kills a couple of days.

—Scott Spencer

### 734

What I like in a good author is not what he says, but what he whispers.

—Logan Pearsall Smith

### 735

The best writers make the fewest words go the longest way.

—Anonymous

### 736

The meaning of a writer will be found not just in what he intends to say, or what he does literally say, but in the effect of his writing on living things.

—Howard Zinn

### 737

Everybody is writing, writing, writing—worst of all, writing poetry. It's be better if the whole tribe of the scribblers—every damned one of us—were sent off somewhere with tool chests to do some honest work.

—Walt Whitman

### 738

A writer can do nothing for men more necessary, satisfying, than just simply to reveal to them the infinite possibilities of their own souls.

—Walt Whitman

### 739

The Six Golden Rules of Writing: Read, read read, and write, write, write.

—Ernest Gaines

### 740

Writing is easy. All you do is stare at a blank sheet of paper until drops of blood form on your forehead.

—Gene Fowler.

### 741

For me, writing is foremost a mode of thinking and, when it works well, an act of discovery.

—Joseph Epstein

### 742

I have written so much about my myself because I am the subject on which I am the best informed.

—Samuel Butler

### 743

Writing should be the settlement of dew on the leaf.

—Ralph Waldo Emerson

### 744

Let the reader find that he cannot afford to omit any line of your writing because you have omitted every word that he can spare.

—Ralph Waldo Emerson

### 745

Writing a book is an adventure. To begin with it is a toy and an amusement; then it becomes a mistress, and then it becomes a master, and then a tyrant. The last phase is that just as you are about to be reconciled to your servitude, you kill the monster, and fling him out to the public.

—Winston Churchill

### 746

Forget your personal tragedy. We are all bitched from the start, and you especially have to be hurt like hell before you can write seriously. But when you get the damned hurt, use it—don't cheat with it.

—Ernest Hemingway

### 747

The chief glory of every people arises from its authors.

—Samuel Johnson

### 748

A writer who is afraid to overreach himself is as useless as a general who is afraid to be wrong.

—Raymond Chandler

### 749

Beauty is that at which a novelist should never aim, though he fails if he does not achieve it.

—E.M. Forster

### 750

I don't believe that less is more but that more is more, that less is less, fat fat, thin thin, and enough is enough.

—Stanley Elkin

### 751

The writer is essentially investigating himself, always trying to reprogram the responses to his own history.

—John Gregory Dunne

### 752

A character or an idea has to grow like a seed and take possession like one's own development and passage through life.

—Daphne du Maurier

### 753

If a writer does not respond to his own past—never mind that he may not understand it—then I suspect he can never be a very good writer.

—John Gregory Dunne

### 754

Never write a biography of anyone whose children are still alive.

—Scott Donaldson

### 755

It's like driving a car at night. You can never see further than the headlights, but you can make the whole trip that way.

—E.L. Doctorow

### 756

Lying is the beginning of fiction.

—Jamaica Kincaid

### 757

The proper study of mankind is books.

—Aldous Huxley

### 758

The good end happily, and the bad end unhappily. That is what Fiction means.

—Oscar Wilde

### 759

Fiction reveals truths that reality obscures.

—Jessamyn West

### 760

In writing fiction, every sentence is its own reward.

—Amy Tam

### 761

Fiction is higher autobiography.

—Alberto Moravia

### 762

In order that people may be happy in their work, these three things are needed; they must be fit for it; they must not do too much of it; and they must have a sense of success in it—not a doubtful sense, such as needs some testimony of other people for its confirmation, but a sure sense, or rather knowledge, that so much work has been done well, and fruitfully done, whatever the world may say or think about it.

—John Ruskin

### 763

Tormented by the cursed ambition always to put a whole book in a page, a whole page in a sentence, and this sentence in a word. I am speaking of myself.

—Joseph Joubert

### 764

My ambition is to say in ten sentences what everyone else says in a book—what everyone does *not* say in a book.

—Friedrich Nietzsche

### 765

The problem is to teach ourselves to think, and the writing will take care of itself.

—Christopher Morley

### 766

The secret of good writing is telling the truth.

—Gordon Lish

### 767

The essence of writing is to know your subject.

—David McCullough

### 768

Writers have to get used to launching something beautiful and watching it crash and burn. They also have to learn when to let go control, when the work takes off on its own and flies, farther than they ever planned or imagined, to places they didn't know they knew. All makers must leave room for the acts of the spirit. But they have to work hard and carefully, and wait patiently, to deserve them.

—Ursula K. LeGuin

### 769

My niece said to me, "I want to be a writer."
I said, "Are you sure?"

—Beth Greene

### 770

The gift of expression is not the same as that of conception: the first makes great writers; the second, great minds.

—Joseph Joubert

### 771

Write straight into the emotional center of things. Write toward vulnerability. Don't worry about appearing sentimental. Worry about being unavailable; worry about being absent or fraudulent. Risk being unliked. Tell the truth as you understand it. If you're a writer, you have a moral obligation to do this. And it is a revolutionary act—truth is always subversive,

—Anne Lamott

### 772

I aim to give to those who read me strength, joy, courage, defiance, and perspicacity—but I take care above all not to give them directions, for I feel that they can and must find them by themselves. I was about to say: in themselves.

—Andre Gide

### 773

I never make my books: they grow; they come to me and insist and being written.

—Samuel Butler

### 774

It is by sitting down to write every morning that one becomes a writer.

—Gerald Brennan

### 775

It took me fifteen years to discover that I had no talent for writing, but I couldn't give it up because by that time I was too famous.

—Robert Benchley

### 776

The original writer is not one who imitates nobody, but one whom nobody can imitate.

—Chateaubriand

### 777

That writer does the most, who gives his reader the most knowledge, and takes from him the least time.

—C.C. Colton

### 778

First we eat, then we beget; first we read, then we write.

—Ralph Waldo Emerson

### 779

By writing quickly we are not brought to write well, but by writing well, but by writing well we are brought to write quickly.

—Quintillian

### 780

I'm always looking for the author who can lift me out of myself.

—Henry Miller

### 781

A good rule for writers: do not explain overmuch.

—W. Somerset Maugham

### 782

The waking mind, you see, is the least serviceable in the arts. In the process of writing one is struggling to bring out what is unknown to himself. To put down merely what one is conscious of means nothing.

—Henry Miller

### 783

You can't be a serious writer of fiction unless you believe the story you are telling.

—Norman Mailer

### 784

Why use a modifier to set straight a not-quite-right noun when the right noun is available?

—William Safire

### 785

Write while the heat is in you.

—Thoreau

### 786

How vain it is to sit down to write when you have never stood up to live!

—Thoreau

### 787

Sentences which suggest far more than they say, which have an atmosphere about them, which do not merely report an old, but make a new impression: to frame these, that is the art of writing.

—Thoreau

### 788

I hate commas in the wrong places.

—Walt Whitman

### 789

Avoid detailed descriptions of characters.

—Elmore Leonard

### 790

You always find things you didn't know you were going to say, and that is the adventure of writing.

—John Updike

### 791

It takes a heap of sense to write good nonsense.

—Mark Twain

### 792

There is no royal path to good writing; and such paths as do exist do not lead through neat critical gardens, various as they are, but through the jungles of self, the world, and of craft.

—Jessamyn West

### 793

In certain trying circumstances, urgent circumstances, desperate circumstances, profanity furnishes a relief denied often to prayer.

—Mark Twain

### 794

Writing is a little like a quiet explosion in your head.

—Maurice Sendak

### 795

Ain't it hell the way a book walks up to you and makes you write it?—don't you feel almost predestinarian?

—Carl Sandburg

### 796

*Manuscript*: Something submitted in haste and returned at leisure.

—Oliver Herford

### 797

We should try to be the parents of our future rather than the offspring of our past.

—Miguel de Unamuno

### 798

Technique is noticed most markedly in the case of those who have not mastered it.

—Leon Trotsky

### 799

With but very few exceptions, every writer whose published work you have read and relished managed to capture your attention only after taking a fearsome beating of the ego.

—George V. Higgins

### 800

Vigorous writing is concise. A sentence should contain no unnecessary words, a paragraph no unnecessary sentences, for the same reason that a drawing should have no unnecessary lines and a machine no unnecessary parts. This requires not that the writer make all his sentences short, or that he avoid all detail and treat his subject only in outline, but that every word tell.

—William Strunk, jr.

801

As to the Adjective: when in doubt, strike it out.

—Mark Twain

802

Avoid clichés like the plague.

—Anonymous

803

Writing is difficult only when you are good at it.

—Lyndon Felt

804

Putting aside the need to earn a living, I think there are four great motives for writing, at any rate for writing prose.

1. Sheer egoism. Desire to seem clever, to be talked about, to be remembered after death, to get your own back on grownups who snubbed you in childhood, etc. etc.

2. Aesthetic enthusiasm. Perception of beauty in the external world, or, on the other hand, in words and their right arrangement.

3. Historical impulse. Desire to see things as they are, to find out true facts and store them up for the use of posterity.

4. Political purpose. Desire to push the world in a certain direction, to alter other people's idea of the kind of society they should strive after.

—George Orwell

805

Everything's got a moral, if only you can find it.

—Lewis Carroll

### 806

The road to hell is paved with adverbs.

—Mark Twain

### 807

Bad writers plagiarize; good writers steal.

—George V. Higgins

### 808

It is only by not paying one's bills that one can hope to live in the memory of the commercial classes.

—Oscar Wilde

### 809

If in one hundred years I am only known as the man who invented Sherlock Holmes, then I will have considered my life a failure.

—Arthur Conan Doyle

### 810

I am still of opinion that only two topics can be of interest to a serious and studious mood—sex and the dead.

—W.B. Yeats

### 811

I've been rich and I've been poor. It's better rich.

—Gertrude Stein

### 812

I write a book for no other reason than to add three or four hundred acres to my magnificent estate.

—Jack London

### 813

The only demand I make of my reader is that he devote his whole life to reading my works.

—James Joyce

### 814

Never do anything yourself that others can do for you.

—Agatha Christie

### 815

Being a cult figure in one's own lifetime, I am afraid, is not at all pleasant.

—J.R.R. Tolkien

### 816

The past is never dead. It's not even past.

—William Faulkner

### 817

Always do sober what you said you'd do drunk. That will teach you to keep your mouth shut.

—Ernest Hemingway

### 818

Money is the barometer of society's virtue.

—Ayn Rand

### 819

Men can starve from a lack of self-realization as much as they can from a lack of bread.

—Richard Wright

### 820

In the US, you have to be a deviant or die of boredom.

—William Burroughs

### 821

There's nothing that makes you so aware of the improvisation of human existence as a song unfinished. Or an old address book.

—Carson McCullers

### 822

There is a marvelous peace in not publishing.

—J.D .Salinger

### 823

Great things are not accomplished by those who yield to trends and fads and popular opinion.

—Jack Kerouac

### 824

If you really want to disappoint your parents, and don't have the heart to be gay, go into the arts.

—Kurt Vonnegut

### 825

If there's a book you really want to read, but it hasn't been written yet, then you must write it.

—Toni Morrison

### 826

The worst enemy to creativity is self-doubt.

—Sylvia Plath

### 827

If you do not seek to publish what you have written, then you are not a writer and you will never be.

—George V. Higgins

### 828

A poet never takes notes. You never take notes in a love affair.

—Robert Frost

### 829

Before they made tools, perhaps before they made trouble, men and women were busy at the loom of fiction, looking for clues to becoming more human.

—Wright Morris

### 830

The great myth (and barrier) for creative people is the belief that their creativity precludes them from being organized. The reality is that their disorganization can get in the way of their creativity.

—Odette Pollar

### 831

I belong to the faction holding that divulging pieces of long fiction still in process can be detrimental to their prospects of completion....It is very difficult to tell a story twice, both times successfully.

—George V. Higgins

### 832

Any given writer can fool any given reader except one on any given day; the one he cannot trick is himself.

—George V. Higgins

### 833

The words in prose ought to express the intended meaning, and no more; if they attract attention to themselves, it is, in general , a fault.

—Samuel Taylor Coleridge

### 834

You *Do* Have Enough Talent.

—Jack M. Bickham

### 835

No tears in the writer, no tears in the reader.

—Robert Frost

### 836

Chaos in the midst of chaos isn't funny, chaos in the midst of order is.

—Steve Martin

### 837

One writes to teach, to move or to delight.

—Rodulphus Agricola

### 838

Writers, like teeth, are divided into incisors and grinders.

—Walter Bagehot

### 839

My entire soul is a cry, and all my work the commentary on that cry.

—Nikos Kazantzakis

### 840

A word is not the same with one writer as with another. One tears it from his guts. The other pulls it out of his overcoat pocket.

—Charles Peguy

### 841

Fiction never exceeds the reach of the writer's courage.

—Dorothy Allison

### 842

If the wisdom of the rich consists in what the rich want to hear and think about themselves, it is not surprising that the rich nation confers its richest rewards on those who can preserve the illusions of innocence.

—Lewis Lapham

### 843

The whole duty of a writer is to please and satisfy himself, and the true writer always plays to an audience of one. Let him start sniffing the air, or glancing at the Trend Machine, and he is as good as dead, although he may make a nice living.

—E.B. White

### 844

Writing is the only thing that, when I'm doing it, I don't feel I should be doing something else.

—Gloria Steinem

### 845

For a long time now I have tried simply to write the best I can. Sometimes I have good luck and write better than I can.

—Ernest Hemingway

### 846

Writing is like prostitution. First you do it for love. Then you do it for a few friends. Finally you do it for money.

—Moliere

### 847

Experience counts in this line of work; one does not become a professional in this generation of writers without having first served a protracted, often painful, almost always unpaid novitiate. Still Moliere's analogy mostly holds: until you get a few dents in you, the chances that you will write a story that impinges on the marrow of the reader are not very good.

—George V. Higgins

848

Uncommon things must be said in common words.

—Coventry Patmore

849

An artist is his own fault.

—John O'Hara

850

If a young writer can refrain from writing, he shouldn't hesitate to do so.

—Andre Gide

851

Men for the sake of getting a living forget to live

—Margaret Fuller

852

Substitute "damn" every time you're inclined to write "very", your editor will delete it and the writing will be just as it should be.

—Mark Twain

853

Work is the means of a living, but it is not living.

—Josian Glibert Holland

854

There is nothing laudable in work for work's sake.

—John Stuart Mill

855

It is no light thing to have secured a livelihood on condition of going through life masked and gagged.

—John Morley

856

Hemingway, after all, in 1929 had only the automobile, the train, the streetcar, the movies, the gramophone, and radio to keep his potential readers too occupied to read him. Your competition, especially television, is stronger, far wealthier, more insistent, and omnipresent, and the people in position to buy work from you are acutely aware of it—it competes for their time too.

—George V. Higgins

857

The more words the less wisdom.

—Anonymous

858

No man but a blockhead ever wrote, except for money.

—Samuel Johnson

859

I have never written a "good" line, but the moment after it was written it seemed a hundred years old.

—Oliver Wendell Holmes

860

Read over your compositions, and whenever you meet with a passage which you think is particularly fine, strike it out.

—Samuel Johnson

861

When I feel inclined to read poetry, I take down the dictionary. The poetry of words is quite as beautiful as that of sentences.

—Oliver Wendell Holmes

862

It is the glory and the merit of some men to write well, and of others not to write at all.

—La Bruyere

863

Writing is an excellent means of awakening in every man the system slumbering within him.

—Georg Christoph Lichtenberg

864

Characters make their own plot. The dimensions of the characters determine the action of the novel.

—Harper Lee

865

Readers of novels are a strange folk, upon whose probable or even possible tastes no wise book maker would even venture to bet.

—E.V. Lucas

866

A man would do well to carry a pencil in his pocket and write down the thoughts of the moment. Those that come unsought are commonly the most valuable and should be secured because they seldom return.

—Francis Bacon

867

My first notebook was a Big Five tablet, given to me by my mother with the sensible suggestion that I stop whining and learn to amuse myself by writing down my thoughts.

—Joan Didion

868

Joan Didion is a whiner.

—Lyndon Felt

869

Gin and water is the source of all my inspiration.

—Lord Byron

870

Whatever satisfies the soul is truth.

—Walt Whitman

871

The one thing that is necessary, in life as in art, is to tell the truth.

—Leo Tolstoy

### 872

I estimate (based on some rough numbers from the Library of Congress) that humanity now publishes as many words every week or so as it did in all human history up to 1800.

—James Gleick

### 873

Novels, even good ones, can be read simply to pass the time; music, even the greatest, can be used as background noise but nobody has yet learned to consume a poem: either one cannot read it at all, or one must listen to it as its author intended it to be listened to.

—W.H. Auden

### 874

A poet is a liar who always speaks the truth.

—Jean Cocteau

### 875

All fiction for me is a kind of magic and trickery—a confidence trick, trying to make people believe something is true that isn't.

—Angus Wilson

### 876

Better to write for yourself and have no public than to write for the public and have no self.

—Cyril Connolly

### 877

Happy is he who writes from the love of imparting certain thoughts and not from the necessity of sale— who writes always to the *unknown friend*.

—Ralph Waldo Emerson

### 878

There is a better way for everything. Find it.

—Thomas Edison

879

More writers fail from lack of character than from lack of intelligence.

—Ezra Pound

880

A limited vocabulary, but one with which you can make numerous combinations, is better than thirty thousand words that only hamper the action of the soul.

—Paul Valery

881

Words are the small change of thought.

—Jules Renard

882

I want to escape the unrest, to shut out the voices around me and within me, and so I write.

—Franz Kafka

883

A writing mentor of mine once said that it takes a million bad words to get to the good words. While that can be frustrating to aspiring writers, the reality is sometimes we need to work on writing and developing the skill. A basketball star doesn't get their by dreaming about the game and talking about their favorite players. They get there by spending hours on the court practicing their free throws. Don't allow the time it has taken you to become a frustration. Instead, let it be an indication of the devotion you have to your dream of publication.

—Tiffany Colter

884

The hardest thing to learn in life is which bridge to cross and which to burn.

—David Russell

### 885

It is impossible to imagine Goethe or Beethoven being good at billiards or golf.

—H.L. Mencken

### 886

The only immortal soul man has is the lasting impression he makes on other men's minds.

—P.W. Atkins

### 887

A man who dares to waste one hour of time
has not discovered the value of life.

—Charles Darwin

### 888

Keep your exclamation points under control. You are allowed no more than two or three per 100,000 words of prose.

—Elmore Leonard

### 889

The difference between the right word and the almost right word is the difference between lightning and the lightning bug.

—Mark Twain

### 890

Between the one-syllable humors of the comic strip and the anemic subtleties of the literateurs there is a wide stretch of country, in which the mystery story may or may not be an important landmark.

—Raymond Chandler

### 891

Writing is a form of prayer.

—Franz Kafka

### 892

To write that essential book, a great writer does not need to invent it but merely to translate it, since it already exists in each one of us. The duty and task of a writer are those of a translator.

—Marcel Proust

893

Syllables govern the world.

—John Seldon

894

The only thing one can give an artist is leisure in which to work. To give an artist leisure is actually to take part in his creation.

—Ezra Pound

895

Invention requires an excited mind; execution, a calm one.

—Johann Peter Eckmann

896

When a book, any sort of book, reaches a certain intensity of performance it becomes literature. That intensity may be a matter of style, situation, character, emotional tone, or idea, or half a dozen other things. It may also be a perfection of control over the movement of a story similar to the control a great pitcher has over the ball.

—Raymond Chandler

897

I think that trying to puff a small story into a big book is a mistake. Books and short pieces of fiction should be permitted to find their own proper length.

—John D. MacDonald

898

Just as you waddle up to the true relations of the cosmos, your vocabulary blurs.

—Norman Mailer

899

You have to fall in love with hanging around words.

—John Ciardi

### 900

Poor writing is…a symptom of inhibition and nervousness. Better English is the language spoken and written by someone who feels at ease.

—Rudolf Flesch

### 901

Art is a lie that makes us realize the truth.

—Pablo Picasso

### 902

A poem begins in delight and ends in wisdom.

—Robert Frost

### 903

The sad truth is, for most authors, their first novel will never be published. That is because it is more of a practice piece than a well thought out story. In fact for many their first two or three books may never actually end up on a bookshelf. This should not discourage you, however. Instead, start the process again. Think up new plotlines and characters. It is the brainstorming that keeps writing exciting and your excitement and your excitement that will keep your writing fresh.

—Tiffany Colter

### 904

You can't be a dilettante writer….You have to get a routine going. Routine becomes a rhythm.

—Thomas Thompson

### 905

Writing's a job. Sit your ass down and do it.

—Lyndon Felt

### 906

Nobody asked any one of us to become a writer.
No one will care if you don't become one.
No one but you, that is.

—George V. Higgins

www.ingramcontent.com/pod-product-compliance
Lightning Source LLC
Chambersburg PA
CBHW070535290526
45790CB00002B/511